Identity and Diversity in New Music

Identity and Diversity in New Music: The New Complexities aims to enrich the discussion of how musicians and educators can best engage with audiences by addressing issues of diversity and identity that have played a vital role in the reception of new music but have been little-considered to date.

Marilyn Nonken offers an innovative theoretical approach that considers how the environments surrounding new music performances influence listeners' experiences, drawing on work in ecological psychology. Using four case studies of influential new music ensembles from across the twentieth century, she considers how diversity arises in the musical environment, its impact on artists and creativity, and the events and engagement it makes possible. Ultimately, she connects theory to practice with suggestions for how musicians and educators can make innovative music environments inclusive.

Marilyn Nonken is a concert pianist, musicologist, and Associate Professor of Music at New York University.

T0347733

CMS Emerging Fields in Music
Series Editor: Mark Rabideau
DePauw University, USA
Managing Editor: Zoua Sylvia Yang
DePauw University, USA

The *CMS Series in Emerging Fields in Music* consists of concise mono-graphs that help the profession re-imagine how we must prepare 21st Century Musicians. Shifting cultural landscapes, emerging technologies, and a changing profession in and out of the academy demand that we re-examine our relationships with audiences, leverage our art to strengthen the communities in which we live and work, equip our students to think and act as artist-entrepreneurs, explore the limit-less (and sometimes limiting) role technology plays in the life of a musician, revisit our very assumptions about what artistic excellence means and how personal creativity must be repositioned at the center of this definition, and share best practices and our own stories of successes and failures when leading institutional change.

These short-form books can be either single-authored works, or contributed volumes comprised of 3 or 4 essays on related topics. The books should prove useful for emerging musicians inventing the future they hope to inhabit, faculty rethinking the courses they teach and how they teach them, and administrators guiding curricular innovation and rebranding institutional identity.

Identity and Diversity in New Music
The New Complexities
Marilyn Nonken

For more information, please visit: www.routledge.com/CMS-Emerging-Fields-in-Music/book-series/CMSEMR

Identity and Diversity in New Music
The New Complexities

Marilyn Nonken

New York London

First published 2020
by Routledge
605 Third Avenue, New York, NY 10017

and by Routledge
2 Park Square, Milton Park, Abingdon, Oxon, OX14 4RN

First issued in paperback 2020

Routledge is an imprint of the Taylor & Francis Group, an informa business

Library of Congress Cataloging-in-Publication Data
Names: Nonken, Marilyn, author.
Title: Identity and diversity in new music : the new
  complexities / Marilyn Nonken.
Description: New York, NY : Routledge, 2019. | Series: CMS
  emerging fields in music | Includes index.
Identifiers: LCCN 2019015673 (print) | LCCN 2019015879
  (ebook) | ISBN 9780429758232 (pdf) |
  ISBN 9780429758218 (mobi) | ISBN 9780429758225
  (epub) | ISBN 9781138388482 (hardback : alk. paper) |
  ISBN 9780429425516 (ebook)
Subjects: LCSH: Music—Social aspects—History—20th
  century. | Music—Social aspects—History—21st century. |
  Music—20th century—History and criticism. | Music—21st
  century—History and criticism. | Verein fèur musikalische
  Privataufffèuhrungen. | Group for Contemporary Music. |
  Itinâeraire (Musical group) | Bang on a Can All-Stars.
Classification: LCC ML3916 (ebook) | LCC ML3916.
  N65 2019 (print) | DDC 780.9/04—dc23
LC record available at https://lccn.loc.gov/2019015673

ISBN 13: 978-0-367-72771-0 (pbk)
ISBN 13: 978-1-138-38848-2 (hbk)

Typeset in Sabon
by Apex CoVantage LLC

For Goldie Celeste and Billie Swift.

Contents

Preface

In 2014, the College Music Society's Task Force on the Undergraduate Music Major (TFUMM) produced a provocative report entitled "Transforming Music Study from its Foundations: A Manifesto for Progressive Change in the Undergraduate Preparation of Music Majors" (Sarath, Myers, and Shehan 2016, 45–85). Asking "What does it mean to be an educated musician in the twenty-first century?", the task force questioned assumptions of the basic undergraduate music curricula and proposed radical revisions, distinguishing between what has traditionally been seen as foundational musical knowledge ("skills and concepts representing those dimensions of music understanding that transcend time and place, that are inherent in the nature and structure of music, and that may be referenced descriptively across eras, styles, and cultures") and other kinds of flexible knowledge ("that which may be fluid in relation to change in musical worlds beyond academe") (Myers 2016, 297). The TFUMM manifesto emphasized that the educated twenty-first-century musician must not only understand the universal or transcendent aspects of the musical art but also grasp the ephemeral, transient cultural factors that can both enhance and inhibit musical life. The ideal music curriculum serving this musician would offer practical as well as foundational knowledge, including the tools to navigate emerging technologies, platforms, and sociological networks related to performance and pedagogy; to finesse interdisciplinary interactions; and to surmount today's formidable global divides.

The task force identified creativity, diversity, and integration as core pillars of this ideal curriculum. These three elements were not defined, although the report acknowledged that "fleshing out these definitions might, in the future, be essential to implementing TFUMM's proposals" (Sarath, Myers, and Shehan 2016, 51).

Vagueness and inspecificity pose a hindrance to progress. Speaking to the issue of cultivating new audiences, the manifesto quotes flutist Claire Chase, the force behind the International Contemporary

Ensemble. "Nurturing new audiences is a shared responsibility of all those claiming the profession of music." "Artistry, engagement, and entrepreneurship are inseparable." These words are inspirational, and inspirational statements like these appear in the mission statements of many fine organizations, which similarly seek "to tear down barriers and cultivate an active spirit of invitation" (New Music Gathering, founded 2014), "facilitate an ecosystem of creativity through music . . . to make composers, and the music they create, a vibrant and integral part of our culture" (American Composers Forum, founded 1973), and "to broaden experience, knowledge, and enjoyment of every style of new music by embracing the full range of today's compositional activity and giving voice to music that might otherwise not be heard" (Boston Musica Viva, 1969). But making statements does not make change. Aspiration may be a step toward achievement, but it is not a reliable guarantor. Even for those who seek progressive change, it can be difficult to translate ideals and recommendations, however well-intended, into actions with positive or even predictable results.

Reaching broader audiences and fostering cultural diversity in a meaningful way, with a serious commitment to diversity, inclusion, and equity, require more than simply exploring revised curricula, alternative venues, and innovative programming strategies; despite the potential benefits of a sharply raised consciousness, "good intentions and sound business practices cannot overcome a history of social and economic segregation" (Carnevale and Smith 2016, 140). *Identity and Diversity in New Music* is thus an attempt to flesh out working definitions of creativity, diversity, and integration and to suggest how we might approach these complex issues in relation to our musical activities, with an eye toward being specific, pragmatic, and real.

I must acknowledge the inspiring role of Lisa Coleman, Senior Vice President for Global Inclusion, Diversity, and Strategic Innovation at New York University, whose words convinced me that the time was right to pursue this project. Thanks also to Mark Rabideau for his encouragement and enthusiasm and for not being justly alarmed by the messiness of my topic. For their camaraderie and willingness to comment on work-in-progress, I am grateful to my colleagues at New York University Tristan McKay and Manuel Laufer. Special thanks to the wonderful people at Easton's Nook Writer's Retreat, particularly Nadine Mattis, for providing me the peace and quiet to get my thoughts together. Most of all, I am grateful for the love and support of George Hunka.

References

Boston Musica Viva. "About Boston Musica Viva." Boston Musica Viva website. https://www.bmv.org/about (accessed May 22, 2019).

Carnevale, Anthony, and Nicole Smith. "The Economic Value of Diversity." In *Our Compelling Interests: The Value of Diversity for Democracy and a Prosperous Society*, edited by Earl Lewis and Nancy Cantor, 106–57. Princeton: Princeton University Press, 2016.

Myers, David E. "Creativity, Diversity, and Integration: Radical Change in the Bachelor of Music Curriculum." *Arts and Humanities in Higher Education* 15, no. 3–4 (2016): 294–307.

Sarath, Edward W., David E. Myers, and Patricia Shehan Campbell. *Redefining Music Studies in an Age of Change: Creativity, Diversity, and Integration*. New York: Routledge, 2016.

Series Editor's Introduction

Music is embraced throughout every culture without boundaries. Today, an increasingly connected world offers influence and inspiration for opening our imaginations, as technology provides unprecedented access to global audiences. Communities gather around music to mourn collective hardships and celebrate shared moments, and every parent understands that music enhances their child's chances to succeed in life. Yet it has never been more of a struggle for musicians to make a living at their art—at least when following traditional paths.

The College Music Society's *Emerging Fields in Music Series* champions the search for solutions to the most pressing challenges and most influential opportunities presented to the music profession during this time of uncertainty and promise. This series re-examines how we as music professionals can build relationships with audiences, leverage our art to strengthen the communities in which we live and work, equip our students to think and act as artist-entrepreneurs, explore the limitless (and sometimes limiting) role technology plays in the creation and dissemination of music, revisit our very assumptions about what artistic excellence means, and share best practices and our own stories of successes and failures when leading institutional change.

These short-form books are written for emerging musicians busy inventing the future they hope to inherit, faculty rethinking the courses they teach (curriculum) and how they teach them (pedagogy), and administrators rebranding institutional identity and reshaping the student experience.

The world (and the profession) is changing. And so must we, if we are to carry forward our most beloved traditions of the past and create an audience for our best future.

Mark Rabideau

Introduction

In 2016, deep sea biologists discovered something particularly unique about snails living in the ocean off the coast of Antarctica. The hard-shelled mollusk known as *Gigantopelta chessoia*, surviving in a most inhospitable environment—a sunless underwater terrain characterized by scorching hydrothermal vents; terrific pressure; and strong concentrations of hydrogen sulfide, methane, and heavy metal—was observed undergoing a dramatic internal metamorphosis. Once the snail had reached a certain level of maturity, its digestive system stopped growing. It ceased grazing for food. Its teeth, stomach, and intestine moved aside, making way for the radical expansion of its esophageal gland, which quickly grew to the extent that it took up most of its body. This organ was then colonized by bacteria, which multiplied and thrived in its sheltered environment. From that point on, these bacteria provided the snail with a lifetime's supply of food. "Housing them internally appears to promote additional adaptations," wrote the authors of the study, noting the "close-knit relationships" of the hosts and their guests (Chen et al., 2017). In a remarkable example of parallel evolution, the snail's adaptation to the hostilities of its environment ultimately optimized the organism's access to its limited nutrients.

Those dedicated to performing and presenting new music in America may feel as if they, too, are foraging for scraps in something akin to the unforgiving ocean floor. "New music groups generally are born and die each year like mayflies," wrote Donal Henahan of *The New York Times* in a 1981 review of Speculum Musicae, "and most leave just about as much evidence behind of ever having existed." Audiences, the musician's lifeblood, can be elusive. Government and private support for the arts is unreliable; in 2017, the president of the United States proposed eliminating both the National Endowment for the Arts and the National Endowment for the Humanities, and local agencies and private foundations are often strapped for resources. It requires tremendous energy to maintain basic standards of performance and integrity while remaining fiscally viable as an organization or financially stable as an independent artist. Those dedicated to presenting new musical works face the added pressures of cultivating audiences for unfamiliar composers, securing venues attractive to audiences and affordable within their budget constraints, connecting with funders and presenters willing to take chances on emerging voices, and establishing relationships with sympathetic advocates, promoters, and critics. Well-trained musicians, no longer a rare commodity, face a chronic shortage of gigs, teaching jobs, and performance opportunities. Yet the awareness of imbalances within our own environment—that gnawing sense that the agendas of educational institutions, the professional opportunities that await trained musicians, and the public's listening preferences are "seriously misaligned" (Freeman 2014)—has been with us since the earliest years of the twentieth century. This angst, rather than exceptional, has been a malady from which most musicians dedicated to new work suffer. It's our own First World Problem, our disease of the rich. While this is a serious concern, we might benefit by reconsidering this imbalance as neither catastrophic nor fatal but as an environmental circumstance to which we can adapt by fostering change, within ourselves and in the world around us.

Could we, like our friend the snail, adapt? We might then reorient ourselves to the complex systems in which we find ourselves engaged. Rather than seeing ourselves as victims of larger forces, we might turn the outside in, conceiving new environments for musical listening and in so doing foster robust communities in which diverse musical organisms would have a better chance of thriving. I'll address these issues from an ecological perspective, emphasizing the direct and mutual relationships of musical organisms, and consider how diversity and identity relate to the professional lifespan of the twenty-first century musician.

My perspective has been influenced by the writings of the philosopher Martin Seel, who describes aesthetic experiences ecologically, as providing contexts for intense contemplation and imagination. Whether Seel writes about music, painting, sculpture, or literature, he always focuses on the agency of the perceivers, who actively engage with and are transformed by the energy of the artwork (Seel 2005, 152–53).

> We can react aesthetically to anything and everything that is anyway sensuously sensuously present. There are places where it is difficult *not* to behave aesthetically (depending on one's

inclination, in the forest or in the garden, at an auto dealership or in a museum, in a concert hall or in a sports area), just as there are places where it is difficult to do so: in an office of a public authority, in a parking garage, during an examination, at the dentist's, or at Wal-Mart.

(Seel 2005, 35)

Yet whether we enter into the aesthetic environment actively or passively, either arbitrarily or with intention, we experience great aesthetic moments—in nature, art, or sport—as things that shake, enrapture, stun, or captivate us.

That the power of the musical experience lies in this mutual exchange of energies had become clear to me as a performer long before I'd encountered Seel's writings. As a pianist dedicated to music of the past hundred years and particularly the repertoire created within my own lifetime, I've long seen the musical environment an ecosystem. As a freelancer in New York, I saw my work unfolding not so much in a field defined by contrasting genres, aesthetics, and movements as in an environment defined by the actions and interactions of many diverse agents (performers and composers, listeners and presenters, administrators, funders, critics), all interacting as driven by their particular orientations, wants, and needs.

I attribute my deepest attachment to the ecological metaphor (if it is indeed metaphorical) to two performances of music by Morton Feldman and John Cage in which I took part. In October 2002, at New York's Merkin Hall, I first performed Feldman's *Triadic Memories* (1987). It was not only my debut performance of the ninety-minute work but also my first solo recital at Merkin; the pianist David Holtzman, scheduled to perform Stefan Wolpe's *Battle Piece* (1947) that evening, had been forced to cancel. I was asked to play at the last moment. Under any circumstances, it's an intense experience to perform Feldman's music. This particular evening, I felt particularly focused, every second suffused in the resonance of the sound in the space. I was intensely aware of every small sound in the auditorium, as if each rhythmic and timbral nuance were magnified and amplified. After the performance was over, amid the general hubbub, an audience member, unknown to me, approached. He was as enthusiastic as I was exhausted. Having come to the hall after a long workday, he'd felt stressed, aggravated by traffic and the daily indignities of life in Manhattan. He'd come to the hall full of tension. Then, gradually, he relaxed into the piece. It was quite different from the music that he'd been expecting. He'd become entranced by its intricate patterns and undulating rhythms . . . mesmerized . . . until . . . he'd fallen asleep.

I wasn't sure what to make of this. Then, he told me, He'd woken up. And he was still in the piece. For him, it was a revelation. For me, this was revelatory as well, because this performance had provided him something precious: a valuable respite, a shelter from the storm. It wasn't just a piece to be understood or a masterwork to be appreciated. *Triadic Memories* was a place he went, from which he emerged energized and elated. From that point on, I began to see my performance not as an opportunity to present, interpret, or recreate "great works" or even to communicate a message but as an opportunity to create places of sanctuary.

In 2003, I was invited to perform at Cleveland's AKI Festival, curated by the innovative organist Karel Paukert and percussionists Paul Cox and Allen Otte. The festival coincided with a production of Cage's *Musicircus* (1967) at the Cleveland Museum of Art, which was then hosting an exhibit of Jasper Johns's *Numbers*. All day, musical performances took place throughout the Museum, in specific galleries and at predetermined times. By design, it was agreed that all of the performers involved would stop whatever they were doing at exactly 4:33 in the afternoon, wherever they were, and perform Cage's 4'33" (1952). When the time came, I found myself essentially alone in a small screening room. There was only one person in the hall, whom I could see out of the corner of my eye as I sat at the piano. I recall beginning the performance with trepidation, feeling the strange intimacy of the situation, as the essential contract of performance was so explicit. As performer and listener in this exposed environment, we had specific roles to fulfill. No small amount of trust was required to see the performance through to the end; at any point, either one of us could have chosen to turn away, but we saw the work through. After the performance was over, the listener stood, and he clapped. I bowed. At that moment, I felt a rush of gratitude for the listener's commitment and a flooding recognition of this reciprocity. Again, the act of performance was not about interpreting, presenting, or even representing, but the aesthetic experience was defined rather by the energy and dynamics of the environment, in a performance act that celebrated powerful forces of mutuality. Both listener and performer were actively engaged and directed, not just perceiving the music "as a piece" but bonding together to create the very environment in which 4'33" was realized. This reciprocity and personal contact, this honest exchange, is in no way something exclusive to a particular repertoire. While there might not be much to "hear" in Cage's composition, for me, this performance would come to exemplify an ideal musical experience

Identity and Diversity's discussions run toward the world of contemporary music, as it is my area of professional specialization and the game that I have played with the most success thus far. I've been fortunate to explore the world of new music from many positions: as a performer, administrator, scholar, teacher, and audience member. I've worked with composers at different stages of their careers, and I've seen how the most exciting musical projects can revitalize and energize not only individuals but entire communities. Some composers flourish and others flounder, not because of the content of their music but because of how they engage with and capture the hearts and minds of their communities. My work as a musicologist explores how traditions of the past inform today's performance practices, and I continue to be fascinated with how today's attitudes toward the new in music are influenced by developments in science and technology as well as factors such as race, gender, ethnicity, education, and class. As Artistic Director of Ensemble 21 from 1992 until 2005, a non-profit contemporary music performance group based in New York, and as a board member of organizations such as the Fromm Music Foundation and Composers. Now, I've been a grant-seeker and a grant-giver. I've witnessed how financial, political, and demographic factors influence which musicians get funded and how. Now, directing Piano Studies at a highly diverse university in a sanctuary city, I'm aware of how the choices we make as musicians reveal the cultural values we hold dear and the principles upon which we rely.

I've also seen, with dismay, half-hearted and uninformed attempts toward diversity and inclusion regularly fail. These attempts are often misguided and, at worst, made in bad faith. And while the point of this book is not to point fingers, I have seen first-hand disingenuous nods toward inclusion that risk doing more damage to the field than good. A new music performance group that includes only the names of the women composers it programs in its materials, omitting the names of all male composers in hopes of appearing more "diverse" to potential funders. An award-winning chamber ensemble that programs original works by emerging voices in what appears a generous outreach gesture, only to throw the scores in a backstage garbage can. An aspiring duo that describes their peripatetic touring lifestyle online as "homeless and happy," only to suffer a violent social media backlash and accusations of cultural insensitivity. And there's the venerable organization that details an educational initiative online, citing a partnership with a local charter school offering music classes and composition workshops, providing composer-mentors for youth of color and bridging the worlds of opera and hip-hop . . . which sounds impressive, until one realizes that the program has been dormant since 2004.

While fair and inclusive treatment of women (cis and trans), at-risk youth, and the poor are admirable goals, these forms of misrepresentation erode the trust of audience, performers, patrons, and creative staff. Such occurrences, all of which can be documented, betray undiagnosed malignancies.

David Myers, an author of the TFUMM report, summarized some of his concerns:

> Increasingly, in a complex world, musicians must be leaders and problem-solvers. They must advance opportunities for music engagement across social and societal sectors influenced by age, race, cultural and ethnic backgrounds, education, socioeconomic level, professional priorities, and technology. Such ambitions entail intersecting issues of producing a livable income, assuring value and respect for diverse musics through participatory engagement, acquiring knowledge and skills to create and perform an array of musics authentically and artistically, and initiating creative ventures for the public good . . .
>
> [A]s musicians educated in more relevant ways transition into the professional world, the ecosystem that incorporates professional and community music organizations, freelance musicians, and higher education will become more relevant to societal concerns and thus more widely valued as a societal necessity.
>
> (Myers 2016, 297)

This book will focus on two core components: the concept of a musical ecosystem and the processes of adaptation by those who populate the musical environment react to its complexities and, actively and mutually, effect change within it. Bringing together theory and practice, I'll consider the reception of new music in light of contemporary writings on diversity and ecological aesthetics. My hope is to suggest how complex musical environments may function and how, contextually, values can be assigned to elements like creativity, diversity, and integration.

My primary goal is to outline some of the complexities faced by performers, performing ensembles, and presenters concerned with bringing new work to today's listeners and engaging more fruitfully with their communities. Performers and presenters who advocate for contemporary music may be uniquely attuned to these issues. Reaching the audience—any audience—has always been a top priority. Presenting unfamiliar music to listeners always demands certain ingenuity and scrappiness because listeners are never a blank slate; they bring to their listening experiences memories, skills, and preferences, which determine how they respond to new environments. Interdisciplinary endeavors have encouraged performers of new collaborative work to look beyond the "standard" audience for classical music, to those captivated by dance, theatre, literature, the visual arts, fashion, gaming, sports, and social and political causes. The imperative to reach new audiences has almost mandated that new music performers reach across ethnographic, cultural, and social divides. And in so doing, perhaps no one has been more prescient than the performers and presenters involved with computer and electronic music, interactive electronics, acousmatic music, and multimedia work. This community has long recognized the transformative power of technology, not only to bridge communities otherwise unconnected but also to illuminate the psychological processes unique to the musical experience and the nature of sound itself.

My secondary objective is to provide a critical history of influential performing ensembles, assessing their contributions in light of contemporary theories. In our relatively ahistorical era, much can be learned by exhuming extinct musical cultures, as the reception of new music has always been decisively shaped by issues of relating to culture, politics, ethnicity, economics, class, education, and local power dynamics. To achieve crucial equilibria within today's relatively precarious environments of the performing arts, it's important to be aware of the myriad factors that have long figured in the production, presentation, and reception of new music. When we bring matters of diversity and identity into the mix, we muddy already brackish waters. It's helpful to distinguish old from new complexities, bearing in mind composer George Rochberg's words from "The Avant-Garde and the Aesthetics of Survival" (1969): "There is no greater provincialism than that special form of sophistication and arrogance which denies the past, and no greater danger to the human spirit than to proclaim value only for its narrow slice of contemporaneity" (Rochberg 2004, 226).

Today, we can do more to create long-range plans for the kinds of diversity that we want to explore, accounting for the identities and histories of those we hope to involve and the kinds of environments that we want to share with them. Yet we must proceed conscious of the variables at play. "We cannot convene a random collection of diverse people and expect diversity bonuses," warns the social scientist Scott E. Page. "We need a theoretical understanding of whether and how diversity can produce benefit on particular tasks. We need to make reasoned judgments about what type of diversity might be germane to the task at hand" (Page 2017, 2). The journalist Kelsey Blackwell, who writes on social justice and its relation to creative expression, offers similarly cautionary words:

> I challenge this idea that "inclusive spaces" can be made without serious reflection, exertion, and patience. To be a truly inclusive space, it must be created by causes and conditions that allow it to happen organically—the internal work has been done so that the fullness of many different bodies can coexist.
>
> (Blackwell 2018)

If we want to make change, it's imperative to define the task at hand and then identify task-relevant types of diversity. For each task, we must consider how to anticipate and harness diverse, adaptive entities, each with a mind of its own. Composers, performers, or potential audience members (who themselves may be potential performers and composers as well) complicate matters. These independent and interdependent entities interact within complex networks, and the actions taken at a given time and place have reverberations that affect all of us. In the delicately balanced environments of new music presentation, even small gestures and events trigger seismic reactions. Therefore, we must confront the following questions.

How does diversity arise in the musical environment?
How can diversity make arts organizations more productive?
How does diversity impact robustness, creativity, and innovation in the musical community?
What kinds of events and happenings can our commitment to diversity make possible?
How can our understanding of historical performance practices relating to identity, diversity, belonging, and inclusion inform our own curatorial initiatives?

These questions relate to personnel and audience demographics as well as aspects of programming, performance practice, and institutional commitment. To address them, we must refine our understanding of diversity and identity. Our understanding of what "diversity" and "identity" mean, as principles and facts, reflects the depth of our commitment to inclusion and determines the social implications of our work as musicians. We must consider and reconsider not only what we want to say with our music but to whom we most want to say it and how. Our answers to these questions, on both institutional and individual levels, reflect our understanding of these complexities and our willingness to create environments that not only bring the work of contemporary composers to new listeners but also bridge diverse communities and promote social justice.

I intend this book for the individual musician and the ensemble player, the freelancer and the younger performer, and the educator who's curious or who'd like to be more committed. Some solo performers, chamber ensembles, and presenting organizations, due to years of work and hard-won connections, are fortunate to attain secure financial footing, and they enjoy the support of public and private funders, often coupled with multi-year funding from government and corporate investors. Yet the playing field is far from flat. Organizations with budgets of over $100,000 per year reach a kind of critical mass, which endows them with the capacity to plan years in advance, partner with equally stable and successful organizations, and draw upon full-time staff to assist with administration and fundraising. Cultural initiatives assume heightened potency with the support of angel investors; corporate supporters like Delta Airlines, Carnegie Hall, MIT, and the State Department; and financial officers who arrange for gifts of cash and securities, as well as tax-favorable transfers of bequests, charitable trusts, retirement plan assets, and life insurance policies. So when we seek models, we must acknowledge the extraordinary institutional privilege enjoyed by groups such as the Ensemble Intercontemporain (founded in 1976), which in 1978 received a subsidy equivalent to 30% of the total French state budget for contemporary music (Born 1995, 85). For those feeding at the bottom, it's important to recognize the powerful role of selective philanthropists like Phil Lesh, the bass player of the Grateful Dead, whose Rex Foundation supported commissions and recordings for composers, including Elliott Carter, Michael Finnissy, Chris Dench, Havergal Brian, and Bernard Stevens; and Betty Freeman, who personally supported the work of Lou Harrison, La Monte Young, Philip Glass, Steve Reich, Virgil Thomson, Helmut Lachenmann, and Kaija Saariaho. In the world of contemporary music, the terrain is highly variegated. We don't all have access to the same resources. So while robust organizations like Found Sound Nation (2007) and the International Contemporary Ensemble (2001) are models in many ways, this book is designed for those still in the weeds, surviving lower on the food chain. With an eye toward perennial concerns like longevity and fiscal stability as well as creativity, diversity, and inclusion, I'll proceed with an eye toward different kinds of institutional and personal commitments to representation, diversity, equity, and social justice. What's in question are how these commitments can help performing organizations and individual musicians connect with listeners and attain greater relevancy within their community.

Chapter One ("Old Complexities") presents studies of four performing and presenting organizations: the Verein für musikalische

Privataufführungen (Society for Private Musical Performances, founded in 1918), the Group for Contemporary Music (1962), Ensemble l'Itinéraire (1973), and Bang on a Can (1987). These groups offered their performers, composers, listeners, and collaborators very different kinds of musical experiences. They also provide precedents for many of today's contemporary music ensembles. Thumbnail sketches into the workings of these organizations provide a glimpse into the environments they created and the challenges they faced, while evaluating their respective legacies. This provides an opportunity to consider the relationship of new music to academia, the forces of commercialism and commodification, and the public.

Chapter Two ("New Complexities") examines the nature of identity, connectedness, and the concept of the diversity bonus. I draw on the work of Scott E. Page, a professor of complex systems, political science, and economics at the University of Michigan at Ann Arbor. Page has explored how different kinds of diversity foster robustness and innovation and, alternately, can contribute to catastrophe and collapse in complex systems. "By studying diversity and complexity together, we can start to say things about *what kind* of diversity, *when*, and *under what conditions* produces good outcomes (robustness) in systems with *what kinds* of characteristics" (Page 2011, 14). In this chapter, I also consider the work of political scientist Danielle Allen, Director of Harvard University's Edmond J. Safra Center for Ethics. Allen's work considers the vital role of institutions in creating connected societies and bridging disparate populations. She makes crucial points about identity and inclusion and how today's institutions can contribute to social justice. To generalize, we can say that Page is pragmatist and Allen an idealist. Their perspectives, in tandem, suggest two different approaches to the diversity dilemma.

Chapter Three ("Toward an Ecology of New Music") considers the environments in which the reception of new musical work takes place, defining the levels of sound, performance, and project, presenting suggestions for how diversity can be cultivated and considering how issues of diversity and identity can relate to institutional and personal missions, aesthetic stances, and entrepreneurial efforts. In examining the environment and its affordances and processes of perceptual learning, I will refer to Eric F. Clarke, a professor of music at the University of Oxford. Clarke is engaged with the psychology of performance and applications of ecological theory to music perception; in his seminal *Ways of Listening: An Ecological Approach to the Perception of Musical Meaning*, he considers how knowledge and action interact within musical culture. His work encourages us to consider how elements of diversity and complexity have influenced processes of musical adaptation, evolution, and competition, as their consequences include the rise and fall of aesthetics and ensembles and the critical reception of composers and their works. These processes and the variables they comprise ultimately determine which music reaches any community and how: who is heard and who is not. I situate contemporary music-making and curatorial strategies in this ecological framework to provide a nuanced understanding of how diversity, identity, and inclusion have influenced and continue to influence the reception of new music.

Chapter Four ("Keeping It Real") suggests strategies for the expression of organizational and personal artistic goals that define how our activities as performers and presenters relate to the pillars of creativity, diversity, and inclusion. Diversity and identity, as abstractions and facts, will impact the course of our careers. Our conceptions of them consistently influence the choices we make regarding the music we play, for whom we play, and how we play it. Performers must be specific and pragmatic in this task. I ask that we be real, not in a defeatist or fatalist sense but in the most practical sense: to be honest and proceed without the intention to deceive or impress. A real commitment to creativity, diversity, and inclusion mandates that we consider these elements, organically and holistically, in relation to the musical environments we'd like to create.

My title is inspired by The New Complexity, the compositional movement that emerged in the United Kingdom in the 1970s and 1980s. Many composers and performers of my generation became aware of this movement via Richard Toop's "Four Facets of the New Complexity" (1988). In this article, the Australian musicologist, best known for his writings on Karlheinz Stockhausen, interviewed Michael Finnissy (b. 1946), Chris Dench (b. 1953), James Dillon (b. 1950), and Richard Barrett (b. 1959). All spoke frankly about the complacency that had settled around "classical" music and their mistrustfulness of a musical establishment intent on passing down inherited concepts of musical greatness and import. Dench was particularly forceful on this point:

> What I'm really saying is that it provokes in me a distrust of received musical notions of form, content, and what is musically meaningful. When someone says, "Oh, there is enormous profundity in the way that Schoenberg manipulates a particular series," I look at it and say, "But God, that's not a lot more interesting than the inside of my toaster." There *are* very pregnant musical things, but somehow in the past two or three hundred years, we seem to have gone down this false track of thinking that what is musically valid is what is derived directly, historically . . . But of course,

these are culturally-received "meaningfulnesses," and I would like
to go back as best I can to *pre*-cultural "meaningfulness."

(Toop 1988, 19)

Dench's words reveal his awareness of a crucial misalignment among
historical interactional cultures and the realities of contemporary listeners. He did not want to simply accept as a listener, or recycle as a
composition student, what was being fed to him as meaningful music.
He did not want "great" works foisted upon him. He wanted to hear
and write a new kind of music that appealed to his own listening strategies and points of reference as a listener. He was seeing a kind of
music that would grant him agency as a participant in the musical
process, allowing him the opportunity acknowledge the complexities
of his own identity and construct his own meanings and narratives.

The composers of the New Complexity, fascinated by performa-
tive virtuosity, produced meticulously crafted scores that asked their
players to transcend what may have seemed, at first, conceptual or
physical impossibilities. Their notation involves strange meters (such
as 24/10), complicated polyrhythms (67:17), and, often, extremes of
tempo, density, and detail. Many musicians, understandably, first saw
the music of the New Complexity as something forbiddingly difficult
on the page. My own teacher and mentor, the pioneering American
pianist David Burge, readily dismissed it as "self-indulgent complexity and sonic violence carried to an unnecessarily cruel level of intensity" maintaining that "it is difficult to justify this music as either an
intellectual experience or as an emotional one" (Burge 1987, 245).
While many were and still are intimidated by the looks of these scores,
however, their surface complexities were designed to lead toward an
ecstatic performance act and to the contemplation of issues regarding
the nature of accessibility, virtuosity, and expression.

Over the past two decades, this "complex" music has contributed
to profound discussions of notation, virtuosity, and the psychology of
performance, in scholarly periodicals such as *Contemporary Music
Review* and *Perspectives of New Music*, collections such as *Complexity in Music? An Inquiry into Its Nature, Motivation, and Performability* (1990) and *Polyphony and Complexity* (2002), and more popular
sources such as Ivan Hewett's *Music: Healing the Rift* (2003) and Alex
Ross's *The Rest Is Noise* (2007). In 2004, *NewMusicBox* identified
the New Complexity composer Brian Ferneyhough (b. 1943), then on
faculty at the University of California at San Diego, as "arguably the
most influential composition teacher in America today." Indeed, the
composers associated with the New Complexity, as pedagogues, have
influenced a generation of composers newly concerned with issues of

performance virtuosity and accessibility, including Chaya Czernowin (b. 1957), Jason Eckardt (b. 1971), Katharina Rosenberger (b. 1971), and Aaron Cassidy (b. 1976). Their works have also motivated a generation of performers dedicated to expanding the performance practice for their instrument. As time has shown, it was not the idiosyncratic physical appearance of the New Complexity scores that determined their impact but the manner in which the composers associated with this movement confronted performers and listeners, seeking to resensitize both to what ecological psychologists refer to as the "affordances" of the environment.

Of the composers associated with the New Complexity, Finnissy was particularly vocal about treating listeners not as the passive recipients of culturally-received, predetermined "meaningfulnesses" but as active participants in the construction of personal musical meaning. To him, this meant acknowledging their identities and their histories:

> Something needed to jolt the audience beyond the sound. . . . After all, it's human existence we're dealing with, not castles in the air! I've got more important things to think about than complexity of surface. I'm more interested in the complexity of discourse, intriguing dichotomies, parallels, and dialectics. . . . Composing is also about dealing with Memory. Individual memory, collective memory. The decaying and eventual disappearance of what anyone can remember. Scanning, and transmitting from, the Pandora's box of history. The forthcoming past, and the recollected future. I don't think the performer or the audience should be let off the hook either. I'm involving them *more*, not less.
>
> (Finnissy 2002, 71)

More so than the other composers of the New Complexity (from whom he later sought to distance himself), Finnissy's works confront issues of sexuality, religion, violence, and colonialism; homophobia (*Stanley Stokes, East Street 1836*, 1989; *Seventeen Immortal Homosexual Poets*, 1997); pollution (*Red Earth*, 1988); and attitudes toward violence (*My Parent's Generation Thought "War" Meant Something*, 1999). In his use of referential musical materials as well as texts, he appeals to the distinct identities of community members, acknowledging their histories and inviting their responses. And despite the fact that many of his works demand the skills of virtuoso performers, Finnissy has a parallel history of engaging with amateur players. For decades, he has been associated with Contemporary Music for All (CoMA), an organization founded in 1993 to encourage musicians at all levels of ability to participate in the performance of new work.

(Presently, CoMA's online includes at least ten works he has composed for youth and amateur ensembles.) In this sense, the career of Finnissy, also a pianist, conductor, teacher, and former founder of the Ensemble Exposé, offers a model worthy of emulation: a musician engaged not only with fulfilling his musical vision but also with cultivating diverse audiences for his work and addressing political and sociocultural issues about which he cares deeply.

Following his lead, I hope to offer perspectives that will inspire us to imagine how we might involve our audiences "more and not less" and create musical environments that are more inviting, accessible, and equitable.

References

Blackwell, Kelsey. "Why People of Color Need Spaces Without White People." *The Arrow: A Journal of Wakeful Society, Culture, and Politics*, August 9, 2018. https://arrow-journal.org/why-people-of-color-need-spaces-without-white-people.

Bons, Joel, ed. *Complexity in Music? An Inquiry into Its Nature, Motivation, and Performability*. Rotterdam, The Netherlands: Job Press, 1990.

Born, Georgina. *Rationalizing Culture: IRCAM, Boulez, and the Institutionalization of the Avant-Garde*. Berkeley: University of California Press, 1995.

Burge, David. *Twentieth-Century Piano Music*. New York: Schirmer Books, 1987.

Chen, Chong, Katrin Linse, Katsuyuki Uematsu, and Julia D. Sigwart. "By More Ways Than One: Rapid Convergence at Hydrothermal Vents Shown by 3D Anatomical Reconstruction of *Gigantopelta* (Mollusca: Neomphalina)." *BMC Evolutionary Biology* BMC series17 (March 1, 2017): 62. https://bmcevolbiol.biomedcentral.com/articles/10.1186/s12862-017-0917-z.

Finnissy, Michael. "Biting the Hand That Feeds You." *Contemporary Music Review* 21, no. 1 (2002): 71–79.

Freeman, Robert. *The Crisis of Classical Music in America: Lessons from a Life in the Education of Musicians*. London: Rowman & Littlefield, 2014.

Hewett, Ivan. *Music: Healing the Rift*. London: Continuum, 2003.

Mahnkopf, Claus-Steffan, Franklin Cox, and Wolfram Schurig, eds. *Polyphony and Complexity*. Hofhaim: Wolke Verlag, 2002.

Myers, David E. "Creativity, Diversity, and Integration: Radical Change in the Bachelor of Music Curriculum." *Arts and Humanities in Higher Education* 15, no. 3–4 (2016): 294–307.

Page, Scott E. *Diversity and Complexity*. Princeton: Princeton University Press, 2011.

———. *The Diversity Bonus: How Great Teams Pay Off in the Knowledge Economy*. Princeton: Princeton University Press, 2017.

Rochberg, George. *The Aesthetics of Survival: A Composer's View of Twentieth-Century Music*. Ann Arbor: University of Michigan Press, 2004.

Ross, Alex. *The Rest Is Noise*. New York: Farrar, Straus, and Giroux, 2007.

Seel, Martin. *Aesthetics of Appearing*. Translated by John Farrell. Stanford: University of California Press, 2005.

Toop, Richard. "Four Facets of the New Complexity." *Contact* 32 (1988): 4–50.

1 Old Complexities

Four pioneering, historically important contemporary music ensembles—the Verein für musikalische Privataufführungen (Society for Private Musical Performance), the Group for Contemporary Music, Ensemble L'Itinéraire, and Bang on a Can—set the precedent for countless other performing and presenting organizations, many in existence today. Examining this select sample of ensemble-presenters allows us to consider their contrasting missions and methods, curatorial strategies, constituencies, and sources of support. It also allows us to consider, from an ecological perspective, how they influenced and were influenced by the environments from which they emerged. Vienna in the years following World War I offered a different sociological, economic, and cultural environment than post-1968 Paris, just as New York's Uptown scene of the early 1960s differed vastly from the same city's Downtown a decade later. In these diverse environments, some thrived, and others perished. This leads us to consider both the factors that made some of these groups so robust and those that rendered others unable to adapt.

Verein für musikalische Privataufführungen

By the advent of World War I, Arnold Schönberg had already written many of the works for which he is most renowned today: *Verklärte Nacht* (1908), *Das Buch der Hängenden Gärten* (1909), *Erwartung* (1909), and *Pierrot Lunaire* (1912). These compositions broke free from tonality in an expressionistic, dramatically radical style. Audiences greeted them with a mixed reception. Some listeners were confused by the unusual content and forms of Schönberg's compositions and struggled to grasp his embrace of uncertainty, irrationality, emotionality, and moral ambiguity. Proponents of modernism enthusiastically endorsed the complexities of his music, while conservatives dismissed it with malevolence. He was portrayed in the press as both "a remarkable Viennese genius" (Maurice Rosenfeld, *Musical*

America) and "the representative of German musical frightfulness" (Henry T. Finck, *The Nation*), simultaneously messiah and Satan (Feisst 2011, 31). With awkward ties to academia, Schönberg taught privately and struggled financially. When called for military service at the age of forty-two, his private teaching came to an end, and his creative development halted.

Discharged from the military in 1916, Schönberg returned to Vienna. He found it difficult to work amid the shortages of food and fuel, money, and housing. At this low point in his life (he only achieved financial and professional stability in 1925, when he succeeded Ferruccio Busoni at the Preußische Akademie der Künste in Berlin), he developed the idea of the Verein für musikalische Privataufführungen. The Verein's mission was articulated in a prospectus, presumed to be written by Schönberg's student Alban Berg (1885–1935): "to give artists and friends of art a real and precise knowledge of modern music." The Society gave its first concert in 1918. In the next three years, its players presented over 350 performances of more than 150 works, in 117 concerts.

From the beginning, the goal of the Verein was the education of its members. Schönberg conceived of it as an extension of his teaching: as an instrument of education and not propaganda. Its goals were to prepare works thoroughly and to perform them with clarity, insight, and refinement, without emphasizing any particular style or aesthetic. Inspired by his mentor, the conductor and composer Gustav Mahler (1860–1911), Schönberg sought to infuse the work of the Verein with his principles, methods, and cosmopolitan attitudes (Meibach 1984, 7). This meant rehearsing above and beyond the standards of the day. A single concert might be preceded by eight rehearsals, two of them offered during the standard Viennese concert hour (7:30pm). Schönberg devoted himself wholeheartedly to the Verein, to the extent that he composed no significant musical works during the years he devoted to the project.

The Verein was notoriously private, even secretive. Programs were not announced in advance. Publicity of any sort was prohibited. Guests (non-members) were not allowed, and critics were forbidden; those who were allowed to attend the Verein's activities had to pledge not to publish reports of what they had heard or write or solicit criticisms. At concert events, expressions of approval, displeasure, and gratitude—even applause—were not permitted.

Rules for members consisted of paying dues, endorsing the Verein's purpose, and not violating its general protocols. All rehearsals were open to the society's members, who paid on a sliding scale. They were offered half-price scores for purchase and invited to attend rehearsals and lectures by resident composers and musicologists; in this way, they could follow the preparation of the programmed works from their initial readings to final performances and develop an intimate knowledge of each. The members of the society, however, had no say in the programming decisions, which were made by Schönberg and his performance directors Berg and Anton Webern (1883–1945), the pianist Eduard Steuermann (1892–1964), the violinist Rudolf Kolisch (1896–1978), and the musicologists Erwin Stein (1885–1958) and Benno Sachs (1882–1968). This stemmed, in part, from Schönberg's insistence that critical knowledge separated professional musicians from amateurs.

> Schönberg's mistrust of the layman and the denial of his right to judge stemmed from a deep-seated conviction. He repeatedly expressed such doubts, particularly in reference to the Verein where he insisted that the sole judgment of all artistic matters had to be left to the professionals and not to the members at large . . . it would not occur to an amateur to hold forth assertive opinions in discussions with professionals in the sciences—with a physician, chemist, or astronomer. Nor could the dilettante argue self-righteously with a lawyer or mathematician. In the arts, however, particularly in music, everyone appeared as a self-appointed expert.
>
> (Meibach 1984, 32)

Schönberg's attitude toward the listener foreshadowed that of Milton Babbitt (1916–2011), notoriously articulated in his 1958 article "The Composer as Specialist," commonly referred to as "Who Cares If You Listen?" (Babbitt 2011, 48–54). Schönberg's goal was not to provide audiences with music that they already knew and liked, but to broaden the range of what was offered in Vienna in terms of the composers, styles, and nationalities represented on the concert stage. His was an attempt to make up for lost time; it was only in 1918 that the government lifted its ban on "enemy composers," once again allowing the performance of music from the Allied nations of America, England, France, Italy, and Russia. To educate the public in the postwar years meant to acquaint listeners with previously forbidden works, as well as those dismissed by a Viennese musical establishment epitomized by Johann Strauss, the "Waltz King" (notably, four works of Strauss were performed by the Verein and given, as was its standard, twenty-five hours of rehearsal).

The Verein's opening concert featured the fourth and seventh piano sonatas of Alexander Scriabin (d. 1915), the *Prose lyriques* of Claude Debussy (d. 1918), and the Symphony No. 7 of Mahler (d. 1911) arranged for two pianos by Alfredo Casella (1883–1947). Later programs featured compositions of Maurice Ravel (1875–1937), Erik Satie (1866–1925), and Paul Dukas (1865–1935); Stravinsky, Busoni, and Reger; and the Austrians Egon Wellesz (1885–1974) and Erich Korngold (1897–1957), who later found Hollywood fame as an Oscar-winning composer of film music. Alongside Schönberg, Webern, and Berg, composers from underrepresented nations included the Czechoslovakian microtonalist Alois Hába (1893–1973) and Joseph Suk (1874–1935), the disciple and son-in-law of Antonin Dvořák; the Hungarians Béla Bartók (1881–1945), Zoltán Kodály (1882–1967) and Kodály's student Laszlo Lajtha (1892–1963), an ethnomusicologist; the Polish Karol Szymanowski (1882–1937), who had founded the Young Polish Composers' Publishing Company in 1905; and the Dutch Willem Pijper (1894–1947), whose name is still used to refer to the octatonic scale in the Netherlands. Traditional repertoire, programmed alongside the new music, included song cycles, arrangements of symphonies, and sonatas by Beethoven, Mozart, Brahms, Strauss, Wolf, Schumann, and Bruckner.

As its extensive rehearsal schedule suggests, the Verein upheld an extraordinary commitment to excellence in performance. Its performers were hand-picked advocates for the contemporary repertoire, "primarily of the kind that have placed themselves at the disposal of the Society—out of interest to the cause." Virtuosity for its own sake was not tolerated, and musicians who may have seen their involvement in the Society as a networking opportunity ("for whom the performed work is not the primary purpose") were excluded (Meibach 1984, 49). The player's role was to provide a highly specialized but limited service and a performance that would not overshadow the composition.

> The center of interest was to be the music itself, and the performer was relegated firmly to second place. The music was to be protected from the ruinously bad performances that difficult contemporary music generally received because of the organization of concert life, centered upon the standard repertory. Above all, the music was to be withdrawn both from the dictates of fashion, which inflated and deflated reputations arbitrarily, and from the pressures of commercialism.
>
> (Rosen 1975, 65)

The Verein offered a supportive environment intended to foster a sympathetic reception for the composer. Through the Herculean efforts of Schönberg and his colleagues, the Verein met its artistic goals and adhered to its rigid protocols. "In this Verein," wrote David

Josef Bach, chief of the Art Department of the City of Vienna, "artistic achievements were accomplished which cannot be compared with anything similar in Vienna or anywhere else in the world" (Meibach 1984, 240). Even so, the Verein für musikalische Privataufführungen failed after three short years. This was largely due to the inescapable pressures of a wildly spiraling Austrian inflation, which made it impossible to pay for performers and venues. No doubt, the Verein suffered from its self-imposed restrictions on promotion and publicity, severe rules, and shunning of the press. It also withered in the absence of any municipal support. The city government, committed to a socialist orientation, privileged the diffusion of more accessible musical works, increasingly emphasizing the importance of art forms and styles considered readily comprehensible for Vienna's large working class.

Despite the Verein's spectacular flame-out, it inspired many of the contemporary music groups founded in the next several decades. Some of its extraordinary performers emigrated to America before World War II, where they would perform and teach for many decades. These included Steuermann, who taught at the Juilliard School and mentored pianists including Alfred Brendel (b. 1931), Russell Sherman (b. 1930), Jerome Lowenthal (b. 1932), and Kolisch, who taught at the New School, the University of Wisconsin at Madison, and the New England Conservatory (Steuermann and Kolisch were crucial figures during the early years of the Internationale Ferienkurse für Neue Musik at Darmstadt, which remains one of the most prestigious festivals for new music). Another remarkable performer was the pianist Rudolf Serkin (1803–1991), founder of the Marlboro Music Festival (1951), who would teach for more than three decades at the Curtis Institute. Progeny of the Verein were critical to the rise of contemporary music institutions that emerged in the following decades, including the International Composers' Guild (1921), the Prague Society for Private Musical Performances (1922), the International Society for Contemporary Music (1922), the Donaueschingen Festival (1922), the League of Composers-New York (1923), Henry Cowell's New Music Society (1925), the Pan-American Association of Composers (1928), the Copland-Sessions Concerts (1928), Marlboro Music Festival (1951), and the Domaine Musicale (1954). Thus, the attitudes of Schönberg's society became influential internationally, on stages big and small, and its biases propagated by generations of performers.

Were these attitudes elitist? The answer can only be an unequivocal "yes." To those sympathetic to Schönberg, he stands as a defiant figure representative of all composers held powerless in the face of financial crises, insurmountable inequities of class and education, and virulent strains of nationalism and populism. For such a composer to create this Verein, under those circumstances, was a deeply committed act requiring unique sacrifices. Yet Schönberg's was an elitist vision of a jewel box experience available to a select few: the musical equivalent of *haute couture* or *omakase*, with an extraordinary value like that of a rare hot-house flower. Schönberg felt no connection to the broader public, and he made no secret of his views, as articulated five years after the Verein folded.

> I have surely said it often enough already: I do not believe that the artist creates for others. If others want to establish a relationship between themselves and the artwork, that is their concern, and the artist cannot be expected to deny this to them. Although he should! . . . Art for the people: one can also see it in this. Art is from the outset naturally not for the people.
>
> (Auner 2012, 86)

We can compare the hermetic activities of the Verein to the rise, during the same period, of socially pragmatic *Gebrauchsmusik*: the "useful music" associated with Paul Hindemith (1895–1963), Kurt Weill (1900–1950), and Ernst Krenek (1900–1991). The goals and motivations of composers like Schönberg and Hindemith could not have been more different. The Verein's programs were curated for a small and select, or self-selecting, audience. *Gebrauchsmusik* was designed to be appreciated by amateurs, to sing and play for their own pleasure in their own homes. In his biography of Schönberg, Charles Rosen equates the behavior of both elitists and populists with a surrender to the growing commercialism and commodification of music. Proponents of *Gebrauchsmusik* buckled to the pressures of the marketplace by pandering to the broader public, seeking a broadly accessible common denominator. In a diametrically opposed fashion, members of the Verein fled the pressures of the marketplace by withdrawing from the public entirely and relying on virtuoso performers. In hindsight, neither the strategies of the Verein nor those associated with *Gebrauchsmusik* effectively countered or combated music's commercialism and commodification. The whorishness of *Gebrauchsmusik* and the chastity of the Verein were similarly ineffective solutions of desperation.

Rosen suggests that Schönberg, compared with Hindemith, took the more honorable course despite the fact that it led directly to the scrap heap of history. "Schönberg's Society was a solution of despair, but it was (and is) necessary to maintain the ideal that music is performed because musicians wish to write and play it . . ." he wrote. "In any case, the uneasy relation of composer and public today cannot be solved by composers, who must live with it as best they can:

it is the creation of forces far too large for musicians to do anything about" (Rosen 1975, 69). Although this is an incredibly defeatist view, Rosen's words carried and continue to carry a great deal of weight, particularly in the classical music community, coming from not only a performer of note but also the author of highly regarded works such as *The Classical Style* (1971) and *The Romantic Generation* (1995). Due in part to Rosen's ringing endorsement, this tragic view of the contemporary composer remains current. In the popular press, the Schönbergian epitaph is not uncommon. "Herein lies the misery of the modernist composer" wrote Michael Church of *The Independent*, prefacing his 2003 review of Hewett's *Healing The Rift*, "obliged to teach the audience a new language, but inevitably doomed to fail."

In *Stockhausen Serves Imperialism*, written at about the same time as Rosen's biography, Cornelius Cardew (1936–1981), the experimental composer and co-founder of the Scratch Orchestra (founded 1969), articulated a contrasting viewpoint. Cardew spoke forcefully toward the necessity of change in music, with an attitude toward changing society itself. "At that moment when we genuinely confront the 'necessity for change' in society," he stated, "a process of change begins in us, we begin to grow and develop."

> We begin to participate in changing society and our consciousness grows alongside this. So, in terms of the individual human being just as in terms of society at large, the basis of change is internal. Outwardly, he tries to create the favourable conditions for this change to go forward. The revolutionary does not do this by retiring to a cave for cultivation of his immortal soul but by ploughing into the struggle against the old and the obsolete, against the decadent and the degenerate, against the human agents of oppression and exploitation (also in the field of culture and art), knowing that practical activity in this struggle provides the best possible external conditions favouring the development not only of his own personal consciousness, but also the consciousness of the vast masses of people who are materially and culturally oppressed under the present social system. In the struggle against the old and decrepit the new is born.
>
> (Cardew 1974, 68)

A century after the founding of Schönberg's society, issues of populism and elitism in music have become familiar complexities. In the brief flowering of the Verein, we can suggest that cognitive diversity was highly valued. Indeed, the Verein's remarkable accomplishments could be attributed directly to the extraordinary individual capabilities of its personnel. Yet bringing their gifts, or contributions, to a more diverse audience was never an institutional goal. It was not even entertained as a legitimate possibility. There was never an institutional commitment to bring the cultural experience to broader audiences, only a dedication to *l'art pour l'art*. And these very issues regarding the haves and have-nots would continue to problematize the presentation of new music, long after the emancipation of dissonance.

The Group for Contemporary Music

In 1962, the Group for Contemporary Music was founded in New York by a trio of composer-performers: the pianist Charles Wuorinen (b. 1938), the flutist Harvey Sollberger (b. 1938), and the cellist Joel Krosnick (b. 1941). Graduate students at Columbia University, all were enrolled in Otto Luening's seminar for composition; Luening (1900–1996), born to German parents in the Midwest, had studied in Zurich with Busoni and his disciple Philipp Jarnach (1892–1982). Like Schönberg nearly half a century earlier, Luening was dismayed by the lack of standards for the performance of contemporary works. He thus encouraged his students to perform their own music, presenting in-house programs featuring compositions by their peers and teachers. The Group for Contemporary Music evolved under his guidance, becoming the first composer-run new music ensemble at a university in the United States. The Group would become the godfather of a generation of New York contemporary music ensembles including Speculum Musicae, Parnassus, the New Music Consort, the Da Capo Chamber Players, the Washington Square Contemporary Music Society, and the New York New Music Ensemble.

One inspiration for the group was the violinist and impresario Max Pollikoff (1904–1984). Beginning in 1954, Pollikoff had curated concerts at the 92nd Street Y and Town Hall under the title "Music of Our Time." His programs featured the music of young composers, to whom he occasionally offered commissions. In 1956, he organized a series of readings at Columbia, which connected him to Wuorinen, Krosnick, and Sollberger. A zealot as well as impresario, Pollikoff was on a crusade to convert listeners suspicious of contemporary music. "I just didn't want to play American composers," he was quoted in his *New York Times* obituary (1984). "I wanted to play their new, previously unheard work. To get audiences that, by habit, almost abhor the 'new' to hear and appreciate it." The Group for Contemporary Music was born of his missionary spirit.

Another profound influence on the Group was Edgard Varèse (1883–1965), a fierce advocate for composers' rights. A formative figure in American music, Varèse is perhaps best known for early modern works such as *Ionisation* (1931) and *Density 21.5* (1936), as well as his influence on cult figures such as George Crumb (b. 1929), James Tenney (1934–2006), and Frank Zappa (1940–1930). In 1921, Varèse and the harpist Carlos Salzedo (1885–1961) had founded the International Composers Guild in New York, which recognized "the necessity of [composers] banding together and fighting for the right of each individual to secure a fair and free presentation of his work." In 1922, Varèse had founded the German chapter of the ICG in Berlin, which appointed Busoni as its president. The Pan-American Association of Composers was formed in 1926, also due to his efforts. Upon emigrating to the United States and securing citizenship, Varèse became a vital presence at the Columbia-Princeton Electronic Music Center, founded in 1959, where he was a colleague of Babbitt.

Following in the footsteps of Luening, Pollikoff, and Varèse, the Group for Contemporary Music was oriented around the creative process of the composer. Its mission, articulated in detailed concert programs, was to provide "responsible" performances of new work, extensive rehearsals, and dedicated personnel. The performers who played for decades with the ensemble essentially set the standard for what would be considered the Uptown performance practice. They included the percussionist Raymond DesRoches, pianists Robert Miller and Aleck Karis, harpist Susan Jolles, violinists Benjamin Hudson and Paul Zukofsky, violist Lois Martin, cellist Fred Sherry, and bassists Bertram Turetzky and Donald Palma. Sollberger and Wuorinen conducted, as did Gunther Schuller (b. 1925) on occasion. Many of these players remain active today, teaching and concertizing.

The Group's inaugural concert, held on the eve of the Cuban Missile Crisis, featured two trios written for Wuorinen, Sollberger, and Krosnick by Luening and Peter Westergaard (b. 1931), a faculty member at Columbia and student of Babbitt, Roger Sessions (1896–1985), and Walter Piston (1894–1976). The program featured the Chamber Symphony (1962) by Ralph Shapey, a student of Stefan Wolpe (1902–1972), and Karlheinz Stockhausen's *Kreuzspiel* (1951). As a prelude, Thomas Morley's *Christes Crosse* (1597) was offered, establishing a pattern for the pairing of pre-tonal and post-tonal works that distinguished the Group's programs. Apart from the occasional Baroque offering, the first season featured music of Schönberg, Berg, Webern, Stravinsky, and Messiaen; Babbitt and his student Donald Martino (a student of Sessions at Princeton); Isaac Nemiroff (a musicologist and student of Wolpe); Roger Reynolds (then based in Michigan, who had met Sollberger at the Midwest Composers Symposia); and Rochberg (a student of Giancarlo Menotti).

Unlike Schönberg's society, which sought to acquaint its listeners with a broad range of aesthetics from many countries and intentionally did not privilege the works of its founders, Wuorinen's compositions and those of his peers, teachers, and students were the mainstay of the Group's programming throughout its history. Not entirely private, the Group acquired some cachet for its association with Columbia, whose institutional support was made clear in programs: "The establishment of the Group is an expression of the Music Department's belief that the University has an obligation to serve the community by sponsoring the performance of music which is rarely or never given in the conventional concert environment" (Deaver 1993, 21). From 1962 to 1971, continuing to program repertoire in this vein, the Group gave six concerts annually at the McMillin Theatre at Columbia, now Miller Theatre. After that point, when Wuorinen was denied tenure at Columbia and his ensemble evicted from the Morningside Heights campus, the Group performed less regularly. It increasingly devoted itself to recording projects and ultimately ceased activity in 1992. Thirty years after its founding, many of the original founders and first-generation performers had moved on to other projects.

The Group for Contemporary Music was designed to give composers more control over the performances of their own work. To the credit of the ensemble and its directors, the Group succeeded in raising performance standards, creating a meticulously crafted legacy of recordings and promoting an aesthetic often referred to as "American modernism" or the "Uptown avant-garde." Yet over time, the ensemble has become historically linked with issues of elitism and the vagaries of institutional support. In the face of commercialization and commodification, the Group's "solution of desperation" was to seek refuge, financial support, and artistic freedom in the quarantine of academia. The cave to which it retired, however, proved not the safest home.

After leaving Columbia University, Wuorinen asserted that American universities were neglecting the arts and abandoning their commitment to the country's composers. In his 1971 *New York Times* editorial "Are the Arts Doomed on Campus?" he addressed the roles of the artist, performer, and composer in academia.

> A composer composes: that is his role, and that is his value in a university. [. . .] And this places him in the university context in the same fertilizing position as the scientist's, for all the divergence between the two areas of discipline. Just as the universities make constant concessions to the scientific mind so that it can do its own work, so they must to the artistic mind.
> [. . .]

Can he function alone? Of course, the answer depends on the art, but for a composer, the answer is no. He needs performers, he needs theorists and historians to speculate, criticize, and elucidate, and, above all, he needs colleagues. His music cannot sound without the help of others. . . . In short, he cannot, like the painter or writer, disappear in a puff of disgust at the rigidity and stupidity of institutions. Perhaps, in view of the problems the universities are now having, he has just picked the wrong institution.

Wuorinen's editorial echoes Babbitt, who had asserted that "it is only proper that the university, which—significantly—has provided so many contemporary composers with their professional training and general education, should provide a home for the 'complex,' 'difficult,' and 'problematical' in music" (Babbitt 2012, 53).

Wuorinen suggested that smaller conservatories, not universities with complicated interdisciplinary agendas and competing interests, were the real institutional refuge for contemporary music. In some ways, time has borne him out. In recent years, many new music ensembles have emerged from and been sustained by environments offered by the conservatory system, although Ivy League institutions and even smaller state schools without conservatories offer residencies for new music ensembles and impressive contemporary music programs. Many groups, not particularly "academic" in their orientation, have either emerged from college and conservatory music programs or found safe havens there. Some that continue to thrive with academic support include the International Contemporary Ensemble (Oberlin College Conservatory of Music), the Callithumpian Consort (New England Conservatory), Alarm Will Sound and Ensemble Signal (Eastman School of Music), Dal Niente (Harvard University, Williams College, Indiana University, Stanford University), Sō Percussion, (Princeton University, Bard College Conservatory of Music), the Empyrean Ensemble (University of California at Davis), Nodus Ensemble (Florida International University), Yarn/Wire (SUNY Stony Brook), and Eighth Blackbird (Curtis Institute and University of Chicago). Academia also remains home to many influential festivals of new music. These include the Composers Conference (founded at Middlebury College in 1945), the Festival of New American Music (Sacramento State School of Music, which claims more than forty seasons), June in Buffalo (SUNY Buffalo, founded in 1975 by Morton Feldman and led since 1986 by David Felder), the Annual New Music Festival at Bowling Green State University (1980), the Summer Institute for Contemporary Performance Practice (New England Conservatory, 1998), the North Carolina New Music Initiative (East Carolina University, 2001), and NUNC! (Northwestern University, 2015).

The legacy of the Group for Contemporary Music is not entirely clear. Its directors saw the "free and fair" presentation of new work as the composer's right. Wuorinen felt that he and his colleagues were entitled to the artistic freedom, financial support, and brick-and-mortar home the University could provide. The Group for Contemporary Music attempted to colonize the ivory tower, identifying its sheltered environment as an ideally protected place where it might thrive. For years, it benefited first from Columbia's largesse and then from the patronage of the Manhattan School of Music, to the point that it became a target of those who did not enjoy the same degree of institutional support. "If anything," lamented Paul Henry Lang in a published response to Wuorinen's editorial, "Mr. Wuorinen and his group received more support than anyone else—from foundations, from the university itself, from sympathetic deans. . . ." Over time it became clear that the prime beneficiaries of the Group's successes were neither the student population at large nor the general public but its composers, who were rewarded with decades of excellent performances, commissions, and recordings, and the establishment of their field as a respected academic discipline. Ultimately, the agenda of the Group and its leaders could not be reconciled with that of its host.

In some ways, the Group for Contemporary Music remains an admirable model. It also stands as a warning.

Ensemble l'Itinéraire

The Ensemble l'Itinéraire was founded in 1973 by a group of young composers and performers who met at the Paris Conservatoire in the course of their studies with Olivier Messiaen. Tristan Murail (b. 1947), Gérard Grisey (1946–1998), Roger Tessier (b. 1939), and Michaël Lévinas (b. 1949) formed the musical collective L'Itinéraire (The Path), first presenting concerts as a way of realizing their own works as well as the music of those who inspired them. Although L'Itinéraire was founded barely a decade after the Group for Contemporary Music, it emerged in the wake of May 1968, a time in which nationwide protests and violent strikes in France, as well as widespread dissatisfaction with the status quo, seemed harbingers of rebellion, even civil war. The directors of L'Itinéraire, unlike the Group, did not want to be part of the establishment. They embraced the counterculture, a "cultural expression proper to post-industrial society, the emergent social formation of the 1970s (and beyond)" (Drott 2009, 51). Unlike the Verein, which sought to privately educate a small group of passionate listeners, L'Itinéraire proposed a free and open environment for artistic and scientific exchange.

In 1967, John Chowning had discovered the FM synthesis algorithm, and, by the 1970s, spectral analysis had begun to reveal a wealth of detail about the inner life of sounds (Nonken 2014, 64–71). The expanding fields of music perception and cognition and psychoacoustics were offering fresh perspectives on acoustic phenomena that musicians, for hundreds of years, had intuitively sensed but now could analyze and contemplate anew. The musicians of L'Itinéraire, who were soon joined by the composer and theorist Hugues Dufourt (b. 1943), were dedicated to exploring how the fruits of technology could transform composition, performance, and musical perception. *Musique spectrale* emerged from this collective environment not as a school or technique but as an inherently ecological attitude toward artistic and scientific inquiry.

Murail described L'Itinéraire as "a sort of cooperative where young composers could express themselves in complete liberty" (Drott 2009, 41). What distinguished the ensemble was its orientation as a collective, designed to create an environment of freedom: of expression, of performance, and of research for performers, composers, and their listeners. In relation to the ensemble, its composers pursued independent research in acoustics and psychoacoustics, and their academic or scholarly explorations into the science of sound began to influence how they approached their listeners. The highly specific acoustic detail revealed in spectral analysis inspired new notational strategies, which subsequently transformed how they interacted with their performers. Their rhetoric privileged no particular style or technique but rather emphasized the unity of technique and technology and a desire to explore—through composition, research, and performance—the experience of sound itself.

The composers and performers of L'Itinéraire promised an aesthetic alternative to the programming and performance practices of the long-reigning institution of the Parisian avant-garde, the Domaine Musicale. Modelled on Schönberg's Verein, the Domaine had been founded in 1954 by Pierre Boulez (1925–2016). Directed by the charismatic composer-conductor and in residence at the prestigious Théâtre de la Ville, the Domaine was supported by socialites, intellectuals, celebrities, politicians, and members of the intelligentsia. The Domaine, embraced by the elite as well as the *haute bourgeoisie*, had become a self-appointed arbiter of musical taste, introducing the concert-going public to the music of the Second Viennese School, Varèse, and Stravinsky. Directed by Boulez until 1967, the Domaine Musicale established a canon of twentieth-century masterworks and selected those emerging composers it deemed worthy of note.

> [T]he Domaine became a gateway to success for other composers, an arena in which careers were made or broken, since a successful debut bestowed legitimation and recognition. . . . [T]he Domaine programs included older works selected by Boulez to represent the classics of the modern area. But this selection did not reflect extant judgments . . . so much as construct them, creating a canon of great modern works and composers in the postwar vacuum in which none yet existed.
>
> (Born 1995, 79–80)

In 1970, three years after leaving the Domaine, Boulez was given the extraordinary opportunity by Georges Pompidou to design the Institut de Recherche et Coordination Acoustique/Musique (IRCAM). With this came his leadership of the Ensemble Intercontemporain (EIC), founded in 1976 and heavily subsidized by the government.

Positioning itself as part of the counterculture, L'Itinéraire blossomed in backlash to the institutionalized avant-garde of the EIC. Its stance was socially and politically rebellious and vociferously against what it saw as bureaucracy and hierarchical power structures. L'Itinéraire announced, from the start, that its performers and composers would be on equal footing. For this collective of young artists, music would not be neither product nor commodity; for the post-industrial society, it would offer a new erotics of sound. And if L'Itinéraire's overall perspective seems more philosophical than pragmatic, this may have been due in part to Dufourt's training as a philosopher (as well as composer and pianist) and Levinas's dedication to the work of his father, the philosopher Emmanuel Levinas.

In the early seasons, its programs included works for acoustic instruments and live electronics, often with instruments invented by the ensemble members. Messiaen's music, with its brilliantly colored harmonies and timbres, was a focus, but the ensemble also premiered works by composers little known in Paris who were similarly fascinated with musical timbre and transformation, such as the American George Crumb and the Italians Giacinto Scelsi (1905–1988) and Salvatore Sciarrino (b. 1947). Still in existence today, the ensemble has premiered hundreds of works. It maintains its interdisciplinary character as well; in 2018, its season roster not only included performers and composers but also the astrophysicist and poet Jean-Pierre Luminet and the writer Pierre Rigaudière.

Around the same time that L'Itinéraire was founded, individually minded collectives were forming in many countries. In 1976, Iancu Dumitrescu's Hyperion emerged in Bucharest, resisting government-mandated aesthetic criteria and performance regulations; the ensemble, now in existence for more than forty years, has been committed to exploring new notational strategies and performance practices, in works that engage with spectralism, Eastern European folk traditions, and the ancient repertoire of Byzantium. In the Netherlands, Louis Andriessen's Hoketus ensemble flouted convention with its commitment to amplification and unusual instrumentation. Also founded in 1976, Hoketus performed with opposing duos of pianos, electric keyboards, panpipes, saxophones, electric bass guitars, and extensive percussion. Slightly later, in the United Kingdom, resistance to conventional ensembles, notation, and performance practices was seen in the ensembles dedicated to the New Complexity, such as Suoraan, co-founded by composers Richard Emsley (b. 1951) and James Clarke (b. 1957), and Ensemble Exposé, formed by Finnissy, Barrett, and Roger Redgate (b. 1958). In these instances, performers and composers working collectively led away from an institutionalized avant-garde, the canon (the "culturally received meaningfulnesses" to which Dench referred), and the protocols of the concert hall. No longer retreating from the public, these collectives emerged to place greater emphasis on improvisation, notation, technology, and virtuosity. They drew their public to them in a manner that validated the thoughts and processes of the individual. In doing so, they cultivated dedicated communities who embraced their attitudes toward music, technology, psychology, and social change.

Bang on a Can

Founded in New York in 1987, Bang on a Can emerged with a mission to make contemporary music more accessible. The seeds of the project were planted in the early 1980s at Yale University. Martin Bresnick (b. 1946), a then-new faculty member, had started a series of all-night concerts, titled "Sheep's Clothing," which drew the attention of his students Michael Gordon (b. 1956) and David Lang (b. 1957). These concerts featured all kinds of music, some of it political; students were encouraged to bring sleeping bags, and the free-form events evolved as happenings. In 1984, when Julia Wolfe (b. 1958) arrived at Yale, Sheep's Clothing was no longer in existence but legendary nonetheless.

The memories of these all-nighters served as inspiration for Lang, Gordon, and Wolfe when they migrated to New York City two years later. All were dissatisfied with the presentation of new music at the time, which seemed overly restricted by institutional protocols and aesthetic divisiveness. The Uptown scene, from which they felt alienated, revolved around venues such as Lincoln Center, Carnegie Hall, the Metropolitan Opera, and the Juilliard School. In this cosmopolitan and self-consciously intellectual environment, virtuoso ensembles such as the Group for Contemporary Music, Speculum Musicae, and New York New Music supported the American extension of European musical traditions, such as those of Schönberg and his students.

> New music concerts had the aura of academic lectures. The audience was select and serious, the program notes were lengthy and the composers' biographies filled with accolades. The performers looked like they had spent their lives in practice rooms. The 19th-century classical music conventions they employed were formal and distancing.
>
> (Wolfe 2012, 10)

Lang, Gordon, and Wolfe were equally disillusioned with the Downtown scene. Below 14th Street, artists performed in galleries, lofts, and makeshift "alternative" venues, influenced by American experimentalism, conceptualism, and performance art. The recent graduates were turned off by disaffected attitudes; pretentious dress (the ubiquitous black turtleneck); and the proliferation of unrehearsed, improvised music. In a 2010 *NewMusicBox* interview, the composer and critic Kyle Gann recalled:

> When I first came to the Downtown scene, it was so dominated by free improvisation and lots of other musicians couldn't get their music out. Improvisers didn't need to rehearse. They could just run up there with their instruments and start playing. And so it was squeezing out all the other different kinds of music. And I knew lots of musicians who were very unhappy with that scene because it was so dominated that way.

"Neither side was really fun," recalled Wolfe in a 2016 *New Yorker* profile, "and there was a whole new generation of composers who didn't fit in anywhere." Wolfe, Gordon, and Lang sought to create a different kind of listening environment, one in which music from Uptown and Downtown could be heard on the same program, in an atmosphere free from jargon and posturing. They found additional inspiration in the composer-driven ensembles that operated independently of academic and grant-giving institutions, such as Steve Reich and Musicians (founded in 1966), the Philip Glass Ensemble (1968), and Andriessen's Hoketus (1976). The Kronos Quartet, (founded in Seattle, 1973), whose concerts featured elements of jazz, world music, film music, and rock, as well as classics of Webern and Bartók, was also a model. Reich, who had close ties to the artists Sol LeWitt, Richard Serra, and Bruce Naumann, offered entrée to the Exit Art Gallery in SoHo, which agreed to host their musical happening. As the proprietors declined to stay open overnight, the first Bang on a Can concert was a twelve-hour concert that began in the afternoon on Mother's Day, 1987.

The six original performers, whose extroverted performance style differentiated them from more staid uptown counterparts, included the bassist Robert Black, cellist Maya Beiser, pianist Lisa Moore, percussionist Steven Schick, electric guitarist Mark Stewart, and clarinetist Evan Ziporyn. In 1992, these players would form the core of the Bang on a Can All-Stars, a touring amplified ensemble that sought to bridge genres (rock, jazz, ethnic music, the "avant-garde," and multi-media), maintaining BOAC's free-wheeling, consciously anti-elitist stance while aggressively marketing their virtuosity. (While the group remains in existence, only Stewart and Black remain core members.)

From its first concert, the group's programming emphasized minimalism, populism, and diversity. Lang recalls asking, "What would happen if you had the best academic piece, the best static piece, the best minimalist piece, the best improv piece, whatever, all next to each other?" (Gann 1993). Theirs was an endeavor to expand the envelope and to create an environment in which different kinds of music and listeners would be welcomed. To that end, the first marathon featured, among many other works, performances of Babbitt's *Vision and Prayer* (1961), Reich's *Four Organs* (1970), Andriessen's *De Staat* (1976), and Crumb's *Black Angels* (1970), as well as works by Pauline Oliveros (1932–2016), Lee Hyla (1952–2014), John Zorn (b. 1953), and Aaron J. Kernis (b. 1960). Audience members were encouraged to come and go. Beer was served. The formality associated with uptown bastions of Carnegie Hall and Merkin Hall was jettisoned, and there was a concerted attempt to discourage posing or judging. While the scope of BOAC's activities has grown dramatically over the past several decades, the marathon concerts have continued. Maintaining its initial curatorial stance, it has secured international commercial success.

The Bang on a Can Commissioning Fund was initiated in 1997. This initiative, too, resulted from a desire to liberate composers and their collaborators from the obligations of institutional funders and the arduous application process. Donations are solicited from the BOAC fan base, with priority given to musicians without traditional training or even, necessarily, a proven record of composition and performance. The process was designed to discover musical talents working outside, or not yet corrupted by, the musical establishment. In a 2005 interview in *NewMusicBox*, Lang described the rationale behind the Peoples Commissioning process:

> When you apply to a foundation, and you put the composers you want to commission next to all the other composers, the jurors are looking at people's credentials, so what they are excited about and what they want to fund are people who have already demonstrated to the world that they can do it. But it's always seemed to us that if you rely entirely on that kind of composer, the composer already doing exactly what you know they can do, it actually makes it very difficult to refresh the field. The system is set up to not allow in the people who might actually have opinions that would breathe some new life into the field, something that is forward-looking and exciting.
>
> (Sheridan 2005)

In 2002, decades after the first marathon concert, the Bang on a Can Summer Institute at MASS MoCA was founded to pass along the ideals of the original organization to younger musicians. Young musicians come to "Banglewood" with classical training and an interest in contemporary work, and they are nurtured by the BOAC musicians while receiving training in gamelan, African drumming, Latin music, movement, improvisation, and instrument making.

Looking back, Wolfe would acknowledge that, by the first decade of the twenty-first century, BOAC's once revolutionary approach to multiculturalism had become mainstream.

> For this generation of musicians many of the questions we asked, dreams we had, and obstacles we faced in the early years of Bang on a Can are now nonissues. Embracing the clash—the super mega-mash-up of cultures—the mixing of classical and pop, of counterpoint and re-mixes, of gamelan, jazz, scherzos, blues harmonica, home-made instruments, novel tuning systems, sonata form, James Brown, concertmasters and street musicians—is no longer a concept or philosophy or artistic approach—it just is.
>
> (Wolfe 2012, 168)

Today, BOAC has become something of a conglomerate: featuring not only performances by its own All-Stars and guest artists but staging new productions and tours, producing recordings, sponsoring groups (Asphalt Orchestra), organizing arts initiatives (Found Sound Nation), and maintaining a summer festival. The organization, born of academy-trained composers with a distaste for the establishment, has now effectively colonized the ivory tower, with its founders appointed to the composition faculties at major universities (New York University, Yale University, MIT), recipients of top prizes (Pulitzer Prize, MacArthur Award, Guggenheim Fellowship), members of advisory boards, and the beneficiaries of commissions from Carnegie Hall, the Kennedy Center, and the New York Philharmonic.

A positive message for today's performers is that the environment for new music in America has adapted—that due to the vibrant environments to which BOAC as contributed, a special kind of cultural diversity is being embraced both outside and inside the academy. A less charitable perspective on the same situation might suggest that this is not truly inclusivity diversity but cultural appropriation and that BOAC has essentially legitimized a popular and commercially successful smorgasbord approach to cultural borrowing. Considering the complex issues of identity and equitable representation involved, it's imperative to examine who benefits from this "super mega-mash-up of cultures."

If we associate Schönberg's Verein with the birth of modernism and characterize the Group for Contemporary Music as its direct American descendent, then BOAC offered to its predecessors a postmodern retort. Rather than fleeing from commercialization, it developed a commodified musical language by which listeners could signify their identification with commercial musical culture. The ensemble expressed signature attitudes associated with the postmodern attitude (which itself resists the concept of definition) by challenging distinctions between "high" and "low" culture, questioning the exclusivity of elitist and populist values, embracing pluralism and eclecticism, and characterizing their musical repertoire "not as autonomous but as a commodity responsive to cultural, social, economic, and political contexts" (Kramer 2016, 12). BOAC continues to do so with a distinctive lightness, creatively re-working musical traditions previously held separate and paying homage to the originals while not holding them sacred. BOAC unabashedly pursues what has been described as a fundamentally contradictory postmodern enterprise:

> Its art forms (and its theory) at once use and abuse, install and then destabilize convention in parodic ways, self-consciously pointing to both their own inherent paradoxes and provisionality and, of course, to their critical or ironic re-reading of the art of

the past. In implicitly contesting in this way such concepts as aesthetic originality and textual closure, postmodernist art offers a new model for mapping the borderline between art and the world, a model that works from a position within both and yet within neither, a model that is profoundly implicated in, yet still capable of criticizing, that which it seeks to describe.

(Hutcheon 1987, 180)

Summary

This brief lineage of performing ensembles, necessarily incomplete, reveals competing struggles that all musicians dedicated to contemporary music face in one way or another in the pursuit of a dedicated listenership, free curatorial oversight, financial support, and a suitable home. In a general way, it shows a path from inward-facing practices to those that face out and from the establishments of exclusive clubs to the creation of more collective and communal environments.

From the outset, L'Itinéraire and BOAC were more ambitious than the Group for Contemporary Music and the Verein für musikalische Privataufführungen. The former was essentially conceived as an incubator for its composers and the latter as an educational initiative. All of these ensembles faced threats to their existence. Yet while the Verein and the Group perished in their attempts to find refuge far from the madding crowd, L'Itinéraire and BOAC, like the snail *Gigantopelta chessoia*, adapted. They found ways to create communities within themselves, which have provided them, season after season, with an increasingly dedicated and renewable listenership. This great asset—community—has brought with it institutional robustness, longevity, and financial health.

In general, all four of these ensembles and presenting organizations demonstrated a far greater commitment to cognitive diversity than to identity diversity. Cognitive diversity refers to the contrasting skill sets, repositories of information, expertise, and ways of thinking that different individuals bring to the environment. We see how cognitive diversity was important to Schönberg, in his attempts to cultivate a community of performers, composers, musicologists, ethnomusicologists, and dedicated listeners. The environment idealized by the founders of L'Itinéraire was similarly one of mutual intellectual exchange but one designed to be welcoming to those with interests not only in performance and composition but also in psychology, acoustics, philosophy, and other art forms. The concept of cognitive diversity has also been crucial to Lang, Wolfe, and Gordon's evolving conception of

Bang on a Can, which over time has come to more fluidly incorporate practices from popular music and ethnic traditions.

While the historical sketch I've presented suggests a warming trend toward greater cognitive diversity, it does not suggest a similar trend toward greater identity diversity. Identity diversity, as opposed to cognitive diversity, refers to social identities based on race, ethnicity, gender and its expression, sexual orientation, religion, class, age, nationality, and ability (or disability). Cognitive diversity and identity diversity often go hand-in-hand, as those with unique life experiences often acquire unique perspectives and skills. But they are not the same thing. Considering how to foster creativity, diversity, and integration in new music, it's imperative that these different kinds of diversities are not offered as proxies for one another.

More importantly, it's essential to acknowledge their congruent relationship: that identity diversity—the representation of different types and kinds of people—is the only way to ensure that cognitive diversity is not only present in a group but also communicated and encouraged (Page 2017, 230–36). In identity-diverse environments, cognitive diversity becomes more acceptable; it's easier to think "outside the box" and make innovative proposals when there is the perception that different perspectives are welcome. In an identity-homogenous group, cognitive diversity is less likely to be voiced confidently and less likely to be seen by the larger group as relevant and valid. Yet when a different "kind" of person enters the environment, the tenor of the discussion changes. Priorities and rationales, and the manner in which they are articulated, change. The way individuals see themselves and activities also changes when they find themselves introducing or justifying their work to someone they perceive as not already in their corner.

> Even when identity outsiders do not bring divergent viewpoints or cognitive diversity to the table, their *mere presence* can fundamentally change the behavior of the identity majority and enhance group performance. [. . .]
>
> Identity diversity triggers expectations that cognitive diversity may be present in groups and legitimizes the expression of unique perspectives and knowledge from both identity insiders and outsiders. In addition, the presence of social category diversity can decrease conforming to socially similar others in a group, which ultimately leads *everyone* to voice unique perspectives more confidently.
>
> (Page 2017, 235)

For those involved in the performance and presentation of new work, a serious commitment to expanding the audience necessitates an equally serious consideration of the relationship between identity diversity and cognitive diversity. In the following chapter, a discussion of diversity and identity in new music will consider how these factors come into play in today's new music culture—with an eye toward the bodies onstage, in the seats, and in the boardroom.

References

Auner, Joseph H. "Schoenberg and His Public in 1930: The Six Pieces for Male Chorus, Op. 35." In *Schoenberg and His World*, edited by Walter Frisch, 85–125. Princeton: Princeton University Press, 2012.

Babbitt, Milton. "The Composer as Specialist." In *The Collected Essays of Milton Babbitt*, edited by Stephen Peles, Stephen Dembski, Andrew Mead, and Joseph N. Straus, 48–52. Princeton: Princeton University Press, 2012.

Born, Georgina. *Rationalizing Culture: IRCAM, Boulez, and the Institutionalization of the Avant-Garde*. Berkeley: University of California Press, 1995.

Cardew, Cornelius. *Stockhausen Serves Imperialism*. London: Latimer New Dimensions Limited, 1974.

Deaver, Susan Elizabeth. "The Group for Contemporary Music, 1962–1992." DMA thesis, Manhattan School of Music, 1993.

Drott, Eric. "Spectralism, Politics, and the Post-Industrial Imagination." In *The Modernist Legacy: Essays on New Music*, edited by Bjorn Heile, 39–60. Burlington, VT: Ashgate, 2009.

Feisst, Sabine. *Schoenberg's New World: The American Years*. New York: Oxford University Press, 2011.

Gann, Kyle. "After Ugly Music." Village Voice, June 1, 1993.

Hutcheon, Linda. "The Politics of Postmodernism: Parody and History." *Cultural Critique 5*, (Winter 1986–1987): 179–207.

Kramer, Jonathan D. *Postmodern Music, Postmodern Listening*. Edited by Robert Carl. New York: Bloomsbury Academic, 2016.

Meibach, Judith Karen. "Schoenberg's 'Society for Private Musical Performances,' Vienna, 1918–1922: A Documentary Study." PhD diss., University of Pittsburgh, 1984.

Nonken, Marilyn. *The Spectral Piano: From Liszt, Scriabin, and Debussy to the Digital Age*. Cambridge: Cambridge University Press, 2014.

Page, Scott E. *The Diversity Bonus: How Great Teams Pay Off in the Knowledge Economy*. Princeton: Princeton University Press, 2017.

Rosen, Charles. *Arnold Schoenberg*. Chicago: University of Chicago Press, 1975/1996.

Sheridan, Molly. "Behind the Music: The Bang on a Can Peoples Commissioning Fund." *NewMusicBox*, May 1, 2005. https://nmbx.newmusicusa.org/behind-the-music-the-bang-on-a-can-peoples-commissioning-fund.

Wolfe, Julia. "Embracing the Clash." PhD diss., Princeton University, 2012.

2 New Complexities

In November 2001, following the attacks on the World Trade Center in Manhattan, a Universal Declaration on Cultural Diversity was unanimously adopted by the General Conference of the United Nations Educational, Scientific, and Cultural Organization (UNESCO). Article One set the tone for the document's promotion of laudable goals: "As a source of exchange, innovation, and creativity, cultural diversity is as necessary for humankind as biodiversity is for nature." The Declaration asserted that the encouragement and protection of cultural diversity, on global and local levels, would produce wide-ranging and profound benefits. Cultural diversity, "the common heritage of humanity," would be the guarantor of social cohesion and vitality in civil society and the catalyst for economic growth in developing economies and world markets. On an individual level, it would promise a road toward achieving intellectual, moral, emotional, and spiritual satisfaction. Fostering cultural diversity was identified as an ethical responsibility, a commitment "inseparable from respect for human dignity." In the ensuing years, this language—especially relating to ethics and morality—would have ripple effects. At the third annual New Music Gathering (2017), BOAC All-Star Steven Schick advocated for an "externally facing practice" that would enable musicians to "transcend the claustrophobia of the concert hall and imagine our art not as a set of skills, but as an ethical orientation to the world."

> Making music today must be about nothing less than asserting moral force. It must be about how we—we who have so much and who live so fully—can act responsibly in a world where so many have so little. It must be about the voices too faint to hear.

We have been given inspiring statements and strong directives. We have been told that fostering diversity is a moral imperative, and we may recognize this as an ethical responsibility. We've also been told that there are practical rewards to be reaped from the presence of identity and cognitive diversity: greater productivity, enhanced innovation, and more efficient problem-solving. In the environments of musical presentation and performance, diversity can foster robustness, healthy competition, and make for greater interest, and provide for those who inhabit that environment emotional and intellectual gratification. In terms of cultural capital, the benefits of diversity are "inescapable" (Page 2011, 168). Yet it's not always apparent how individual musicians can nurture cultural diversity within their own communities, which are complex systems whose workings are rarely entirely known to, or controllable by, them.

How diversity functions within any environment, and how any environment capitalizes on its own diversities, depends on the principles directing or guiding its growth and behavior. Those who determine the affordances of the musical environment—performers, composers, and those who present them—must first identify the principles that guide their actions, as these will determine whom they reach and how. More than writing a savvy mission statement, this process entails a serious evaluation of our commitments to both art and social justice and honest discussion about whether our commitments are complementary. Even small organizations and individuals must make informed choices to produce or encourage particular outcomes. Are we engaging with diversity as a fact or diversity as principle? Are we distinguishing well-meant appeals to an abstraction from our directed and immediate engagement with our own environments? As was shown in the previous chapter, we face many obstacles in the presentation of new musical work; this endeavor has always faced abundant challenges. In the current climate, however, we must consider how longstanding and durable challenges relate to issues of identity and diversity. Only by doing so will we find ways to ensure that we consciously leverage diversity for its potential benefits in relation to our musical communities so that it does not become detrimental to our larger goals.

In this chapter, I'll discuss types of diversity, connectedness, and bonding. These concepts will be defined with an eye toward understanding issues of diversity and identity at the local and community levels and the processes by which arts groups and individual musicians set cultural agendas for themselves. I'll refer to different musical initiatives, including the long-running Focus! festival at the Juilliard School; New Music: New Audiences (2012–2014), a cultural program supported by the European Union; and Composers Now, the organization founded in 2010 that supports composer residencies and dialogues, presenter partnerships, and an annual festival. These initiatives among others are detailed to highlight best practices, as well as what I see as common mistakes.

Types of Diversity

Complex systems include biological ecosystems, economies, and populations characterized by shared traits, such as these related to geography, genetics, income, education, gender, sexuality, and ethnicity. These complex systems consist of diverse entities who act, interact, and adapt independently. In these environments, structures and patterns emerge over time, but they are not easily predicted or described. As we consider how diversity may function in our own musical communities, we can investigate its critical relationship to three key elements: affordances, preferences, and adaptation.

The term "affordance" comes from ecological psychology and is associated with the writings of James J. Gibson (Gibson 1966; Heft 2001). Affordances are the possibilities for action offered to us by what the environment endows. Affordances are objective components, whose inherent qualities are subjectively determined in relation to the needs of the individual. "The floor affords walking, a cup affords grasping and a chair affords sitting. However, a chair also affords moving and leaning on. So a particular aspect of the environment can offer a multiplicity of possibilities for action" (Rietveld 2016, 928). Seen through this ecological lens, the affordances of any musical environment offer multiple interpretations, all of which depend on the preferences of the listener.

> An ecological approach recognizes that even relatively simple sounds can afford more than one interpretation—and aesthetic objects are deliberately structured so as to exploit this polyvalence. But this in no way undermines an ecological stance: rather, it encourages a detailed and ecologically appropriate examination of the stimulus . . . in relation to the sensitives of the perceiver(s) in question.
>
> (Clarke 2005, 52)

Preferences determine how affordances are construed and how the endowments of the environment are received. Preference is a rich area of inquiry, as what any listener prefers is directly connected to that listener's identity. As will be detailed, that identity can relate to the acquired knowledge that any listener brings to the musical experience (distinguishing the "naïve" and "experienced" listeners often referred to in the cognitive psychological discourse). It also comprises factors relating to race, ethnicity, sexuality and gender, religion, class, age, nationality, and physical ability, which further determine how individuals navigate their environments. Identity and preference are crucial to understanding how the affordances of any environment become contextually meaningful and how any listener adapts to a musical situation. Adaptation is the process by which individual components of the environment evolve, a process by the which the environment itself is transformed through the mutual engagement of its individual components. As the particulars of biological, economic, and cultural complex systems differ, it's at best metaphorical and at worst overly broad to suggest that the functions of diversity translate unequivocally to the environment of music performance and reception. But I suggest that the core functions of diversity are relevant enough, and they valuably prompt us to reexamine our actions and guiding principles.

When we say that we are aiming for "diversity" in our audiences or our programming strategies, we're not always clear about the multiple diversities that exist. A continuum of diversities includes conceptions of a *diversity of type*, *diversity of kind*, and *diversity of assembly*. These three basic categories are fluid and may overlap, yet all have different implications. The goal is to consider the potential and relative significance of these forms of diversity, each of which may have a different kind of impact on the musical environment.

Most of the time, we refer to what is considered *diversity of type*. This indicates a basic difference in the amount of some attribute or characteristic: variations among members of an otherwise similar group. While we commonly to hear references to types of composers, performers, and listeners, as if they were members of a species, we should be critical of this usage. It's a common strategy for new music programming, possibly the least innovative, and potentially the most offensive.

In the context of curatorial strategies and repertoire, contemporary music's ubiquitous theme programs exploit this diversity of type. We might consider concerts celebrating the birthdays of American minimalist composers of the same generation, such as minimalists Steve Reich (b. 1936) and Philip Glass (b. 1937). Programming devoted to the Second Viennese School or spectral music similarly purports to explores a certain "type" of music. There are dramatic differences in the musics of Glass and Reich, of course, as there are among the works of Schönberg, Berg, and Webern, and Murail and Grisey. Yet there are rewards in hearing their works side-by-side. This curatorial stance offers listeners the opportunity for a particularly directed form of perceptual learning, at best encouraging listeners to appreciate the nuances that distinguish the musics of arguably similar composers, in light of their more obvious commonalities. Such an environment offers something of a musical tasting menu, akin to a flight of fine wines or a plate of cheeses.

Programming that privileges diversity of type is also exemplified by featuring composers from a particular culture, even those who within that culture may have different roles and status. The Focus! series at the Juilliard School, founded in 1985 and directed by Joel Sachs, annually offers programs oriented around themes such as "China Today: A Festival of Chinese Composition" (2018), "Japanese Contemporary Music" (2015), and "The British Renaissance: British Music Since World War II" (2013). These programs tend to introduce their composers first in terms of type, ideally as a means of then looking beyond that type to what makes each exemplar unique.

A higher level or more significant degree of difference involves types but refers to *differences in kind*. Considering the listenership for contemporary music, we might compare the audience for contemporary opera to the audience for acousmatic music. These listeners are generally related by their shared interest in "newer" music. Yet there are substantive differences between them, regarding the environments they inhabit and their behavior within them. The audience for the former might seek out performances of Kaija Saariaho's *L'Amour de loin* (2000), Nico Muhly's *Marni* (2017), and Thomas Ades's *The Exterminating Angel* (2016). These large dramatic works premiered at major performing arts centers and festivals, and attending their premieres might require travel and a significant financial investment to secure tickets, premiere seating, and lodging, for relatively rare performances. These audiences might have more in common with classical music enthusiasts who migrate annually, like geese, to hear Wagner's *Ring* cycle at Bayreuth. Ades, Muhly, and Saariaho, aesthetically, are worlds apart, but the preferences of these kinds of listener relate more to medium and genre. The audience for acousmatic music, on the other hand, might seek out festivals of electronic and computer music such as those hosted by the Society for Electro-Acoustic Music in the United States (SEAMUS, founded 1984) and New Interfaces for Musical Expression (NIME, 1995). They might frequent smaller galleries and cultural spaces dedicated to sound art and installations, such as ISSUE Project Room (2003), or prefer to listen through headsets, downloading digital files with which to engage in the acoustic environment of their choice. This listenership prefers a musical environment defined by an entirely different range of affordances than that of their opera-going contemporaries. Both listenerships are audiences for new music, but they are different *in kind*, seeking out specific genres, frequenting distinctive venues, privileging unique listening environments, and accustomed to investing, financially, to a different degree, according to the music with which they identify. Their identities and behaviors within the environment are determined by their preferences. It's more of a challenge to create a musical environment that can bring these kinds of listeners together.

Diversity of assembly refers the composition of the environment itself, which frames the interaction of various types and kinds. This more dramatic form of diversity relates to how the environment is populated, or peopled. It is relevant to the extent that it transforms the processes of interaction and adaptation that take place within it. When different elements are brought into play in the environment, the balances of its endowments and affordances change. This changes the processes of adaptation and reciprocity that can potentially take place. Therefore, it's imperative to think beyond types and kinds to the greater environments we create as performers and presenters, taking a long and hard look at what we can expect to take place within them.

First, let's take a critical look at a project does *not* exemplify diversity of assembly. For nearly forty years, Focus! has brought attention to lesser-known voices, with several seasons devoted to the music of composers from countries underrepresented on programs in America (surveying current demographics, one could reasonably ask whether composers from China, Japan, and England are particularly marginalized). Apart from "China Today" and "Japanese Contemporary Music," we've seen recently "Our Southern Neighbors: The Music of Latin America." While one might want to hold this up as an example of a commitment to diversity in programing, the presence of these composers' music, however, does not actually change the festival environment, the structure of the concert event, or even (and some may disagree) the nature of its basic content. The diversity of a type or kind of music, in this instance, changes neither the musicians onstage (Juilliard students, with an occasional guest) nor the listeners in the audience, the fan base of the New Juilliard Ensemble and Juilliard Orchestra. These concerts function like most traditional concerts of classical music that do not feature Chinese, Japanese, British, or Latinx composers; they take place in traditional Uptown concert halls (Alice Tully Hall and the Peter Jay Sharpe Theatre), present audience members with a written program with copious notes, and involve conventional performance protocols, ranging from standard concert lighting and intermission to attire, applause, and bows. Compositions are performed by classically trained musicians who play in this fashion on many other concerts, many other nights of the week. While we can point to some variation in the programming, the basic workings of the environment are not transformed by the material itself. It's a programming conceit that does not reflect a profound institutional commitment to diversity as a guiding principle.

In the publicity materials used to promote "China Today," this statement by Sachs precedes the composers' biographies.

> Early in 2017, Juilliard president Joseph W. Polisi, with whom I created the Focus! festival in 1985, asked if this year's edition, his last as president, might explore music in China. Fortunately, I had guides for my search in Alex Brose and Wei He, whom Juilliard has selected as the executive director and dean, respectively, of The Tianjin Juilliard School. Their long experience in China was invaluable. They strongly recommended composer Qigang Chen as a primary contact because as director of several nationwide projects, he has encountered many gifted composers. Since we wanted to commission some young composers, I sought suggestions from Chen, He, Brose, and other composers I know. Gradually a list emerged of some 30 composers born after 1980, seven of whom we commissioned.
>
> (The Juilliard School 2019)

As is explicitly stated, the Focus! environment was assembled according to the preferences of conservatory deans, executive director, and president. While one can assume that there was some consideration of the preferences or identities of potential listeners, this isn't part of how the project was presented to the public. Nothing in this rhetoric suggested a compelling rationale for why one might want to focus on Chinese music (apart from its association with the Tianjin Juilliard School) or the music of these particular composers but for the fact that they were young and gifted enough to impress American "experts." No attempt was made to address the extreme political complexities of the present relationship between the United States and China. Nothing in Sachs's prefatory text acknowledged the conflicted experiences of the many Chinese musicians and students who come to the United States and the racial issues faced by Asians and Asian-Americans. This was a lost opportunity to engage with topics absolutely relevant to the world of the conservatory; recent studies on the subject include popular and scholarly contributions ranging from "Asian American Students in American Conservatories: A Statistical and Sociological Study" (Kim 2013) and *The Making of Asian America: A History* (Lee 2015) to Julia Wang's exposé "The Burden of Being Chinese on Campus " (2016), published in *The Atlantic*, and Michael Ahn Paarlberg's think-piece "Can Asians Save Classical Music?" (2012), which appeared in the online journal *Slate*. While the music of these Chinese composers could have been used to assemble an environment for dialogue and exchange, it was not. At worst, this vein of programming gives an impression of sameness and the interchangeability of "other" cultures.

Diversity of types and kinds in programming cannot be equated with the diversity of assembly. When we talk about diversity in terms of designing more inclusive musical environments, only diversity of assembly will effect change and adaptation. It is not enough to simply show that these individuals exist—as when presidential candidate Donald Trump exclaimed, "Look at my African-American over here!"—but to emphasize that they also have something to say to us about the environment in which we are all equally engaged and welcomed.

A positive example of diversity in assembly is New Music: New Audiences (NewAud, 2012–2014). NewAud was a European initiative that involved sixteen national music organizations and more than thirty performing ensembles in seventeen nations, collaborating to develop concert forms and explore ways of disseminating contemporary music. Supported by the European Union Cultural Programme and a grant of more than 500,000 Euros, the Dansk Komponist Forening partnered with presenters, commissioning organizations, and performing ensembles to form cooperative working groups. Proceeding on the assumption that peer learning would stimulate debate on the needs and aspirations of both audience members and performing artists, each group committed to play the repertoire of the other, meet, and cooperate on an international scale, presenting concerts across the continent and connecting with new listenerships. The goal was to expose all involved (audiences, performers, presenters, and administrators) to works, styles, and performance spaces with which they weren't already familiar. As a result of NewAud, more than one hundred works crossed borders, and a repertoire pool of more than three hundred works was assembled online, allowing the participating ensembles access to each other's repertoire.

Cultural offerings resulting from the initiative, documented extensively online, were wildly different. They drew attention to underserved audiences, unexpected performance venues, and lesser-known compositional voices, while offering profound opportunities for artistic and professional exchange. One concert event, held at the Gothenburg Concert Hall, featured the premiere of *Mondgewächse* by the American composer Patricia Alessandrini, whose work engages with issues of representation. *Mondgewächse* featured the Influence Ensemble, which provides performance opportunities for multiply-disabled performers. Playing alongside the professional musicians of the Swedish ensemble Gageego, the commissioning organization, the musicians of the Influence Ensemble created sound using their feet, eyes, and other body parts via a computer interface. The premiere performances engaged a population rarely involved in concert life, either in the audience or onstage, while also exploring the transformation of the relationship between performer and instrument through technology.

NewAud's other offerings included a performance by the HERMES ensemble of Rolf Wallin's *Strange News*, addressing the use of child soldiers in Africa (Antwerp), and the premiere of Kristaps Pētersons' *Mastering of Acoustics*, a work that explored the relationship between sound, architecture, and history and took place in a Soviet-era airplane hangar (Riga). Oslo listeners took in a concert of music by Carola Bauckholt performed by the Cikada Ensemble, while casually eating and drinking with the composer, and an educational program for children, "Kwartludium in Wonderland," introduced listeners as young as four to "even works that their parents would consider as difficult" (Warsaw). Other performances and premieres were realized in parks and discotheques, courthouses, and abandoned factories. These activities were complemented by workshops in which performers and administrators from across Europe came together to share strategies and a two-day conference on audience development attended by administrators, ensemble directors, and managers (Brussels). In this case, the guiding principles of cultural diversity, creativity, and inclusion permeated the overall endeavor, which lasted for two years and was intended to resonate for seasons to come.

In the United States, it is nearly inconceivable that this kind of government support, almost $600,000, would be allocated to a project of the magnitude solely dedicated to contemporary work. (The bi-annual New Music Gathering offers itself as a "collective place for things for things to grow, improve, solidify, and above all get personal," yet it takes place on a much smaller scale and largely adheres to the familiar models of the academic conference and industry trade-show.) Today's performers and presenters dedicated to new music, however, can make valuable gains on smaller and intimate scale. We can still consider how, on a local level, we can engage underserved audiences in meaningful ways, access unused spaces, explore interdisciplinary threads, and bridge with other musical professionals as well as dedicated amateurs. To do so, we must consider how issues of identity define different communities and might play into an ideally connected new musical society.

Identity, Connectedness, and Bonding

As discussed in the previous chapter, identity diversity refers to social identities based on race, ethnicity, gender and its expression, sexual orientation, religion, class, age, nationality, and physical ability. Differences in individual identity also pertain to elements such as family structure and ancestry, education, class, and geographic location; we're as likely to define ourselves by where we are from as how old we are, and this can influence our cognitive diversities. Identity extends to aesthetic preferences, with regard to the forms of artistic expression with which we're most comfortable, including the types of music to which we like to listen. In the past, it was often assumed that some identity traits were innate (that men and women were characteristically different, or Asians and Africans were inherently "not like" Europeans). This essentialism has been largely rejected. Today, it is commonly understood that many qualities of identity are socially constructed, which is why, however well-meaning, a night of music focusing on the "Chinese-ness" or the "British-ness" of a group of composers comes dangerously close to courting essentialism.

In looking at the composers we play or the listeners we'd like to see in our audiences, we cannot assume that we understand something fundamental about identity when we classify and value people on the basis of individual components of their identities. All people have multiple dimensions to their identity. In different contexts, I identify in different ways: as a practicing musician, a professor of music at a major urban university, a woman, a working mom, a transplanted mid-Westerner, a Gen Xer, and a lover of slow atonal music. I do not like to be categorized as just one of these things. Only by respecting the complex identities of those whom we hope to include in our environments will we understand how we might fruitfully engage them. That is, we must try to understand who potential listeners are in all their complexity in order to know why they might be interested in what we do and how we might reach them. This approach absolutely rejects the desire to "convert" listeners—the goal is not to change listeners but to respect them. Rather than seek to change our audiences so that they come to appreciate what we do, we must change our conception of what we hope to share with them, in relation to the larger environment in which we co-exist.

As issues regarding sexuality and gender have come to the fore, the acknowledgement of the complexity of individual identity becomes ever more important. Optimistically, we can note the activities of international organizations devoted to women in contemporary music, such as a Women in Music and the International Alliance for Women in Music (a result of the 1995 merger of the International League of Women Composers, the International Congress on Women in Music, and American Women Composers). Smaller cooperatives include New York Women Composers (1984), the Irish-based collective Sounding the Feminists (2017), and the Yorkshire Sound Women Network (2015), which specifically seeks to provide women and girls access to music technology. Yet as gender and identity have become newly and publicly complex issues, it's crucial to refine our conceptions of identity and acknowledge that our audiences and collaborators, for example, include different kinds of women, not all of whom feel welcome in the environments offered by the aforementioned organizations. This perspective is articulated by Elizabeth A. Baker, the composer, performer, and founder of the Florida International Toy Piano Festival.

> The problem continues when organizations promote "diversity initiatives" using only images of cisgender white women. What these actions and inactions tell women who look like me—women of color, and individuals for whom I am an ally, including nonbinary and queer women—is that our voices and, more poignantly, our faces are not welcome in this conversation. Personally, it has the effect of taking my agency as a woman away from me . . . I understand how the subconscious presentation of diversity framed exclusively as a "middle-class white cisgender woman's problem" has the ripple effect of silencing women of varied ethnic backgrounds and gender identities.
>
> (Baker 2018)

Baker's critique draws attention to the nuanced nature of identity, reminding us that even organizations that mean well risk alienating those they most hope to support. The French Fair Play Network is thus dedicated to connecting artists in the fields of sound art and experimental and acoustic music who identify as female or trans women. Also based in France, Female Pressure is an international network of transgender, female, and non-binary artists working in electronic music and digital media.

Kelsey Blackwell, whose Black identity plays into her discussions of power and privilege, notes that the sheer fact of explicit inclusiveness cannot be equated with inclusivity. Diverse groups are often invited into the musical experience simply to fill seats or satisfy a hollow mission. Too often, these participants are engaged on the basis of their perceived usefulness—as the composers of "China Today!" or "Our Southern Neighbors"—and they are painfully aware of the situation.

> White people often interpret our mere presence in a room as an opportunity to talk about race, and these are not conversations we always want to have . . .

> For anyone who has tried to "invite in" more diversity, you may
> wonder: Why is it so difficult to get Black and brown people to
> show up? The reason is that merely inviting more people of color
> into a space does not in and of itself make that space inclusive. Pat-
> terns of white dominance suffuse the space just like other spaces
> we occupy, only this time, we're calling it "inclusive." That's more
> painful and frustrating than being in spaces that are blind.
>
> (Blackwell 2018)

A meaningful commitment to identity diversity as a guiding principle
entails acknowledging listeners' complex histories and experiences.
They must sense that the musical experience is not just *for* them but
about them. This requires that musical organizations and performers,
while coming to terms with their own histories and goals, extend their
conceptions of identity beyond mere type and kind and acknowledge
the power of broader, fluid, and textured categories of identity. Only
then will they be able to connect effectively with other communities,
in a musical environment in which all feel equally empowered and
respected. Only then we can contemplate connectedness.

Bridging

A connected society is an environment whose members enjoy the
bonds of solidarity and community but are equally engaged in bringing diverse communities together. They are able to maintain and
protect their own identities while establishing personally valuable
relationships with others, across boundaries of difference (Allen 2016,
90–91). Cultural institutions, musical organizations, and individual
performers with committed agendas can work toward creating more
connected societies and bridging disparate populations. This can be
done on the local level, beginning in our backyards.

A serious issue in the presentation of new music is that communities of its strongest advocates tend to be insular. Performers, ensemble members, arts administrators, and devoted listeners are bonded
together through shared interests and preferences. They may share
levels of education, cultural "literacy," and economic advantage.
Artistically, they might be dedicated to the music of certain composer,
style, or specific performance aesthetic. Professionally, they might
hope to create a particular environment for the musical experience
to develop emerging performance practices or to nurture young performers. Their broader mission might involve educating the public,
promoting a specific repertoire, or supporting the creative processes of
composers—but, on a daily basis, they might be hard pressed just to

get by in today's unforgiving gig economy. Many musicians are united by the challenges of balancing their personal practice with teaching, performing, and, often, working a non-musical job on the side simply for financial security. Those who share these experiences form a kind of society in which bonding takes place through the exploration of shared goals and experiences. Bonding results in the establishment of a tightly knit, coherent community.

It's natural that musicians, as they seek audiences for new work, first reach out to groups of people who resemble them and have kindred interests and goals. The first effort to draw an audience almost always reaches out to related groups: family, close friends, and social similars. In the 1990s, it was a bit of a joke that one could attend any number of new music concerts in New York City and see exactly the same listeners in the audience. The insularity of Uptown and Downtown scenes, twenty years ago, was undeniable.

Yet there was, and is, intense gratification in being part of a bonded community. By nature, we are social and insecure animals. Some of our most meaningful personal relationships are born of these bonded communities. These thrive not only in musical environments but also in houses of worship and schools and populations distinguished by ethnicity and sexual orientation. Members of these familial groups recognize and relive something seminal about their origins. So, as much as we see the value in diversity, we are often hesitant to leave our own groups and wary to admit others who are not like us. And the members of other communities, with whom we hope to engage, do not always want to engage with us or be assimilated.

On both sides, it's easy for bonded communities to atrophy and stagnate. There can be inertia. If the relevant social organization has a homogeneous membership—if its members are all performing musicians or listeners who share the same preferences—then the body of knowledge that informs their activities will be limited. When we separate ourselves out by type and kind, we become constrained in our potential by our lack of cognitive diversity. Such self-similar communities to fall into groupthink, making decisions with a high value placed on maintaining harmony and coherence. Sometimes, irrational decisions are made that fly in the face of critical analysis and evaluation. In music, this sameness works to limit our cultural capital, keeping the initiated in and the uninitiated out.

Musicians and presenters committed to concepts of inclusion can consider the ramifications of *bridging*, the bringing together of diverse groups of people otherwise tightly bonded together. Those with a real desire for change must conceive musical environments that will be conducive to producing social relationships through the musical experience and across boundaries of difference. This necessitates a recognition of the deep-seated fear that, in opening up and bridging together diverse groups, we might lose something of the cultural specificity that distinguishes our endeavor in the first place. Many classically trained musicians dedicated to new work, enthusiastic to reach broader audiences, do not want to adopt the postmodern approach, with its self-consciously indiscriminatory, ironic attitude. They've acquired an expert skill-set that they've worked hard to attain; they may not want to physically change what they do with their instruments or, necessarily, their repertoire. These elements define them. Complex musical identities, such as those forged within the conservatory and college music system, can be closely tied to foundational knowledge of the musical art. Music is a practice and ritual that can bind a community of practitioners together. And so, when the conductor Simon Rattle suggests that the musicians of the Berlin Philharmonic rise from their seats and walk around the concert hall, addressing audience members in a new way and "rethinking our notions of excellence," it can be seen as a threat. (In a 2018 *New York Times* exposé, Michael Cooper detailed the resistance Rattle met in his attempts to transform the attitudes of his musicians.) Expert performers don't always want to adjust, to experiment with new performance aesthetics and acknowledge the perspectives of those less familiar and less immediately appreciative of their skills and accomplishments.

While those in the world of new music performance might feel that disinterested listeners are at fault for small houses, it is often the reality that our own cultural institutions and vaunted performers have atrophied in just this fashion. As Seel warns in *Landscapes of Human Experience*, "We cannot allow ourselves to take things too lightly or too easily with regard to our cultural nature" (Seel 2015).

Achieving a connected society, however, does not require that we shed our cultural specificity. Instead, it requires that we scrutinize how we build our social connections. It is possible to recognize the complex identities of all involved, respecting and protecting bonding ties (within our own communities and the communities of others) while maximizing bridging ties.

In 2010, the composer-conductor Tania León (b. 1943) established Composers Now, an organization whose mission is to "empower all living composers, celebrate the diversity of their voices and honor the significance of their contributions to the cultural fabric of society." A well-known and respected figure in New York for decades, León was a founding member of the Dance Theatre of Harlem; she was the Latin American Music Advisor to the American Composers Orchestra (where she founded the "Sonidos de las Americas" Festival), as well as New Music Advisor for the New York Philharmonic. Founding Composers Now, the Cuban-born León hoped to create an organization that would recognize the identities of composers from diverse backgrounds, not just of "contemporary classical" music but also jazz, ethnic-inspired musics, and electronic genres, charting what she referred to as a "sonic journey through the landscape of the arts of our time." The organization cultivates presenter partners in all boroughs of New York City (not just Manhattan and Brooklyn, but Staten Island, Queens, and the Bronx), seeking to enhance accessibility for traditionally underserved populations. The organization is dedicated to involving composers of all genres, ages, ethnicities, genders, and orientations and diversity and inclusion as guiding principles. I enthusiastically endorse its approach to musical community, which differs radically, in terms of its rhetoric, goals, and programs, from that of organizations like the Fromm Music Foundation at Harvard University, which has significantly subsidized the creation and production of new musical work in America since its inception in 1972. As a current Board Member of Composers Now, having also served on the Fromm's Board of Directors (2012–2017), I feel the comparison is fair.

A new music community recognizing its own diversity was in evidence at Composers Now's 2018 Season Opener, an eclectic event that featured appearances by koto artist Miya Masaoka and jazz bassist Rufus Reid; excerpts from a new opera by emerging composer Felix Jarrar (b. 1995); and music of Žibuoklė Martinaitytė (b. 1973), a Lithuanian-born sound artist whose work considers identity and its relation to place. Works by Ami Yamasaki, the Tokyo-based vocalist and interdisciplinary artist, and the New Orleans-born Christopher Trapani (b. 1980), whose work reflects his fascination with regional American folk traditions as well as spectral music, were performed side-by-side. The event, held at The Jazz Gallery, also honored longtime supporters of contemporary music in America. One award went to Frank Oteri, the composer who has edited *NewMusicBox* since its founding in 1999. Another recipient was Cecille Wasserman, a vital patron of organizations including the string quartet ETHEL, founded in 1988 with the mission of building connection and community; Sphinx, the Detroit-based organization devoted to promoting diversity in the arts; and Face the Music, a program for teens based at New York's Kaufman Cultural Center committed to post-genre music by living composers.

Composers Now's boisterous event bridged many communities. Its programming enthusiastically acknowledged the different members who contributed to the robustness of the environment: not only composers of wildly different aesthetics, traditions, and perspectives and their equally diverse interpreters but also innovative administrators, passionate advocates and critics, and dedicated patrons. The Jazz Gallery is a small space. Yet it may have housed, for that evening, all the organisms crucial to creating a well-balanced environment for the reception of contemporary music.

Not every performing organization and individual artist prioritizes connectedness to this extent or has the means to do so. Yet the commitment to inclusion as a guiding principle can be reflected even in small gestures, such as reduced ticket prices and bilingual promotional materials. It can be conveyed through an ongoing dialogue, articulated in different geographical areas and venues, with new populations. It can motivate relationships with community leaders, who can offer new access to their constituencies and connections to likeminded social organizations. These kinds of small gestures are crucial to bridging with communities tightly bonded within themselves.

The Diversity Bonus

In music as in biology and economics, diversity is a force behind innovation. The concept of the "diversity bonus" (Page 2017) relies on linking cognitive diversity—differences in the information, knowledge, representations, mental models, and ways of thinking that individuals bring to the environment—to better outcomes on tasks such as problem solving, planning, and designing. In complex systems, diversity may enhance robustness, or the ability of a system to continue functioning in the face of change.

In the context of a presenting organization, we can imagine how a leadership team comprised of individuals with experience in diverse areas (arts management, finance, education, and marketing) may be more creative in approaching a budget crisis than a team with expertise in only one area. A team of diverse individuals has more potential to innovate, as all members of the team possess perspectives informed by their experience and unique areas specialization. Performers from different institutional backgrounds and geographical origins develop different ideas about performance practice, programming, production, concert protocols, and outreach; brought together, their expertise can lead them, as a group, to develop unprecedented approaches and strategies unique to the situations at hand. This can lead to forays into new neighborhoods, the design of novel concert formats, and the development of pioneering outreach strategies. "Whether one looks at ecosystems, empires, or cities," writes Page, "greater diversity for the most part correlates with greater productivity" (Page 2011, 9).

A common example of a lack of diversity is the Irish Potato Famine. In the mid-nineteenth century, a toxic organism destroyed Ireland's potato crop, the mainstay upon which nearly half of the population relied for daily sustenance. The rural population had largely depended on only two varieties of potato, neither of which was particularly resistant to disease. In the unusually cool and moist weather of 1845, the crop was attacked by late blight and withered, country-wide, in the fields. In the decade that followed, more than one million people died of starvation, typhus, and famine-related disease. Hundreds of thousands fled the country. By the 1920s, due to emigration and falling birth rates, Ireland's population had been halved.

Aware of the benefits of diversity in the environment, some farmers have developed what is known as "polyculture." Polyculture farming offers an alternative to the dependence on and commitment to a single crop ("monoculture") that led to the Great Hunger. Polycultural farms plant multiple crops in the same space in an attempt to imitate the diversity of natural ecosystems and more efficiently use the land. Specific plants encourage the presence of beneficial weeds and sympathetic insects. Within this strategically planned ecosystem, various species of plants and animals have their own roles and goals, and their mutual presence and interaction make for a balanced ecosystem that fluidly adapts to change. (The highly diverse environments cultivated by polyculture farmers may be contrasted with those associated with the agrochemical giant Monsanto, the purveyor of the toxic defoliant Agent Orange and, more recently, the herbicide Roundup. Monsanto and corporations like it propose sustainability and high yields through a combination of monoculture farming and genetic engineering.) From an ecological standpoint, polyculture farming offers not just a metaphor but a model, suggesting the bonuses diversity can provide.

Cultivating polycultures within the worlds of new music will not magically provide instant solutions to long-standing problems, such as those related to audience recruitment and retention and financial insecurity. We can expect tensions. When we bring together disparate groups, they might not always get along. We've seen plenty of strange bedfellows, ranging from Alarm Will Sound and Radiohead to the EIC and Frank Zappa. Sometimes, this works. Sometimes, it doesn't. For whenever we seek to diversify our environment through the introduction of new elements (a new project, ensemble member, administrator, or presenter partner), there is a period of adaptation and learning.

> Diverse groups are often tossed together. They haven't had the benefit of selective pressures. Should we be surprised that they perform poorly? If we constructed an ecosystem by randomly

tossing together some flora and fauna would we really expect it to function? Of course not. We'd expect an initial period of assembly and organization in which many species go extinct. Thus, leveraging diversity requires an understanding of assembly.

(Page 2011, 251)

One such ecosystem is exemplified by Meet the Composer, which went extinct despite its excellent goals and intentions. Funded in 1974 by John Duffy, Meet the Composer was designed to bridge the gap between composers and their public. Duffy, who had studied with Henry Cowell (1897–1965) and Aaron Copland (1900–1990), asserted that the role of the composer was unappreciated and felt certain that the presence of composers onstage would enhance the reception of their music. His vision was to put the living composer in front of the audience. In fulfilling this vision, Meet the Composer was successful, arranging composer-in-residence programs at more than thirty American symphony orchestras. Meet the Composer's most visible practice, however, may have been making small grants to performing ensembles to subsidize composer appearances on programs featuring their music. Typically, composers were welcomed onstage and given the opportunity to say a few words about their work and take questions from their listeners. For their appearance, they were given a token honorarium. At the time, bringing "the living composer" to the fore seemed a dramatic move.

However, in retrospect, the composers' presence did not significantly alter the dynamics of the environment. "The presence of a composer in a situation is always a winning gesture," commented the composer Robert Hall Lewis in a 1990 conversation with radio producer Bruce Duffie, "but for that gain there has to be a receptivity on the part of the people. If you have a lot of people there who are not really interested in the contemporary music scene at all, I'm not sure that a composer is going to have that much effect." Including the composer in this fashion introduced a new element to the environment, yet it may have inadvertently revealed a limited understanding of assembly and even a disregard for the essential reciprocity among those who share the concert space. Often, it didn't generate a sincere dialogue or one with ramifications that extended beyond the moment. Most orchestras dropped their composer-in-residence programs after Meet the Composer's funding was discontinued. As was noted, in Duffy's *New York Times* obituary, none of its initiatives became self-supporting over time.

In 2011, Meet the Composer merged with the American Music Center to form New Music USA. The establishment of this new organization reveals something of how understandings of assembly have evolved. To better understand the diversity of assembly in contemporary contexts, the next chapter will consider the cultural environments that are home to the processes of musical presentation and reception. We'll consider the components of these complex systems—how they are assembled and what they afford—and speculate about the implications, functions, and consequences of different kinds of diversity within them. How do diversities of type, kind, and composition relate to the principles that drive everything from concert programming to marketing strategies? To reap the benefits of complexity, we must grasp how diversity is leveraged in our communities and within those populations to which we desire access.

It is extremely difficult to measure the effects of diversity in complex systems such as economies and biological environments. It is no easier to measure these effects in the context of the environments in which contemporary music is introduced. Yet the fact that diversity and its consequences cannot be quantitatively measured in the contexts of musical reception does not mean that we should not think seriously about it. Therefore, presenting an admittedly qualitative discussion with a strong metaphorical component, I'd like to look at some hypothetical musical environments and speculate as to what diversity might mean in and for these contexts.

References

Allen, Danielle. "Towards a Connected Society." In *Our Compelling Interests: The Value of Diversity for Democracy and a Prosperous Society*, edited by Earl Lewis and Nancy Cantor, 21–105. Princeton: Princeton University Press, 2016.

Baker, Elizabeth A. "Ain't I a Woman Too." *NewMusicBox*, August 8, 2018. https://nmbx.newmusicusa.org/aint-i-a-woman-too.

Blackwell, Kelsey. "Why People of Color Need Spaces Without White People." *The Arrow: A Journal of Wakeful Society, Culture, and Politics*, August 9, 2018. https://arrow-journal.org/why-people-of-color-need-spaces-without-white-people.

Clarke, Eric F. *Ways of Listening: An Ecological Approach to the Perception of Musical Meaning*. Oxford: Oxford University Press, 2005.

Gibson, James J. *The Senses Considered as Perceptual Systems*. Mahwah, NJ: Lawrence Erlbaum and Associates, 1966.

Heft, Harry. *Ecological Psychology in Context: James Gibson, Roger Barker, and the Legacy of William James's Radical Empiricism*. Mahwah, NJ: Lawrence Erlbaum and Associates, 2001.

The Juilliard School. Focus! 2018 Presents "China Today: A Festival of Chinese Composition;" Six Free Concerts From Friday, January 19, through Friday, January 26, 2018. December 21, 2017 Press Release. https://www.

juilliard.edu/news/130926/focus-2018-presents-china-today-festival-chinese-composition-six-free-concerts-friday (Accessed May 23, 2019).

Kim, Jungeun Elle. "Asian American Students in American Conservatories: A Statistical and Sociological Study." Master's Thesis, Peabody Conservatory, 2013.

Paarlberg, Michael Ahn. "Can Asians Save Classical Music?" *Slate*, February 2, 2012. https://slate.com/culture/2012/02/can-asians-save-classical-music.html.

Page, Scott E. *Diversity and Complexity*. Princeton: Princeton University Press, 2011.

———. *The Diversity Bonus: How Great Teams Pay Off in the Knowledge Economy*. Princeton: Princeton University Press, 2017.

Rietveld, Erik. "Situating the Embodied Mind in a Landscape of Standing: Affordances for Living Without Chairs—Materializing a Philosophical Worldview." *Sports Medicine* 46 (2016): 927–32.

Seel, Martin. "Landscapes of Human Experience." *Contemporary Aesthetics*, 13, December 17, 2015. https://contempaesthetics.org/newvolume/pages/article.php?articleID=731.

Wang, Julia. "The Burden of Being Chinese on Campus." *The Atlantic*, August 15, 2016. www.theatlantic.com/education/archive/2016/08/common-ancestry-complicated-present/495665.

3   Toward an Ecology of New Music

Ecological studies of music, which bridge theory, musicology, music psychology, and cultural anthropology, have emerged and become quietly influential in the past thirty years. Recent works of interest and written in an accessible language include Tia DeNora's *Music in Everyday Life* (2000), Nicola Dibben's "What Do We Hear When We Hear Music?" (2001), Eric F. Clarke's *Ways of Listening* (2004), and David Borgo's "Free Jazz in the Classroom: An Ecological Approach" (2007). The shared precedent for this work is the legacy of the American psychologist James J. Gibson (1904–1979). In 1966, Gibson proposed that human perception and the simultaneous perception of meaning result from active engagement with the environment and the opportunities it affords. Diverging radically from the standard cognitive psychological approach, Gibson asserted that human perceptions and actions are not necessarily mediated by cognitive processes, mental representations, memories, schemas, or pre-acquired information but that the needs and goals of the individual determine, at an elemental level, how the environment is perceived and understood. Revolutionary in the late 1960s, Gibson's work today is not uncontroversial.

> Gibson's claim that perception is direct and unmediated virtually stands alone in 20th-century psychology. All other recent theories assume that between stimulus input (sensations, sense data, stimulation, etc.) and psychological outcome (perceptual experience, response, action, etc.) are mediating processes that enrich or otherwise transform this input.
>
> (Heft 2001, 154)

To conceptualize the musical world ecologically is to prioritize the experience and identity of the individual. It is to conceive of music not as a fixed object to be appreciated but a fluid essence with which to interact. The aesthetic environment affords opportunities for sensation, experience, learning, emotional gratification, and relaxation. Yet how any music resonates with listeners relates to how they actively engage with that environment. This is influenced by their attitudes, identities, and preferences. What any music means to its listener results from a mutual connection between the two.

> An ecological stance on this is that meaning arises from the mutuality of object and perceiver, and sounds specify meanings and values for particular listeners, some of which can be mobilized at particular moments. In this way music is implicated in the construction of identities, and in the social and political context of everyday life.
>
> (Dibben 2001, 184)

To emphasize direct engagement with music in the act of listening is not to deny that talking and thinking about music can be meaningful activities. Sometimes, talking about music can be as enjoyable as listening to the music itself. Yet distractions from the musical experience abound. The past several decades have seen an increased focus on the rationalization of new music, in the form of a massive critical and popular discourse. In music academia, heated debates take place over aesthetic influences, performance practices, and compositional methods and techniques. The field of music perception and cognition has produced decades' worth of empirical studies hypothesizing psychological universals and their relation to music as heard. These scholarly discourses are expanding incrementally but inexorably. Voicing perspectives of practitioners in the field, blogs like *I Care If You Listen, Sequenza 21*, and *NewMusicBox* explore music's relation to social, political, and cultural ideologies with daily updates. Popular criticism produces a similarly inexhaustible supply of reviews, profiles, interviews, and critiques, as well as perennial lists of dubious merit, such as "Ten Young Composers Who Are Redefining Classical Music (*Culture Trip*, 2017) and "Nine Brilliant Contemporary Composers Who Prove Classical Music Isn't Dead" (*Mic*, 2014). All of these are of some interest. Yet these resources do not always—and, I suggest, rarely—connect in a transformative way to the moment of intersection between listeners and new music.

Rationalizations do not reliably enhance the perceptual learning of the listener engaging with music at a certain time and in a given space. "Ideologies and discourses, however powerful or persuasive they seem to be, cannot simply impose themselves arbitrarily on the perceptual sensitivities of human beings, which are rooted in (though not defined by) the common ground of immediate experience" (Clarke

2005, 43). Supplementing or enriching the musical experience itself doesn't lead toward enhanced perceptual learning, which can only occur through sensory interaction with the environment. Instead, engagement with these discourses fosters "symbolic cognition," an indirect response to things based on secondary sources Gibson 1966, 91. While we may value these rationalizations, we may benefit more by redirecting our attentions to the musical environment itself. In our attempts to assemble diverse, equitable, and inclusive spaces for our listeners, we must consider how to facilitate perceptual learning within them, to heighten our listeners' immediate engagement with the music.

Ecological psychology encourages us not to underestimate the immediacies and significance of the musical encounter.

> The cognitive approach to music perception taken by most music psychologists has led to a rather cerebral view of musical activity, where performers and composers attempt to "communicate" musical structure or mood to listeners, who passively decode these structures and then respond with appropriate behaviours.
>
> (Windsor and de Bézenac 2012, 103)

Yet essence of the musical experience and how it becomes meaningful is tied to active perceptual learning: how the listener, in the moment of lived experience, becomes sensitive to the affordances of the musical environment and interprets them in a personal way. Perceptual learning refers to a process of acquiring knowledge *of* the environment, not knowledge *about* the environment. It is a personal practice through which listeners learn what the environment affords them.

All musical experiences involve a degree of perceptual learning, which occurs regardless of genre or style. Performers, presenters, and educators who focus on introducing listeners to new music face the special task of establishing environments specifically designed foster perceptual learning. But how do we facilitate perceptual learning when connecting with new listeners in environments that are unfamiliar and potentially confusing or threatening? Rather than designing tightly controlled environments in which predictable outcomes are the goal, we might instead focus on creative ways to facilitate learning in contexts shaped and negotiated by all participants. Instead of creating a situation engineered to produce a predetermined outcome, we must establish listening contexts in which audience members feel comfortable exploring new ideas and experimenting together, one in which notions of "experts" and "gate keepers" are abandoned in favor of the more engaged and interactive roles of mentors or facilitators (Borgo 2007, 69).

To this end, I'd like to take apart some of the complex musical environments peopled by musicians, listeners, and other agents of culture.

Three nested environments of interaction will be detailed: sound, performance, and project. An ecological conception of sound will be considered in relation to the affordances of two very different works: John Zorn's *Cobra* (1984) and Georg-Friedrich Haas's *In Vain* (2000). Performance will be examined as a frame for the experience of sound. Finally, an examination of "Julius Eastman: That Which Is Fundamental," a production of the Philadelphia-based presenting organization Bowerbird, will consider the complexities of larger projects and their relation to curatorial oversight and institutional commitments.

Sound

Every experience offers its listener a unique environment to explore, defined most fundamentally by the presence of acoustic sound itself. Not all music is made up of things conceived as "pieces," or composed or notated works. Improvisations, chance works, and various trans-media experiences incorporate musical elements but need not be conceived as musical compositions. But we still engage with the world of sound within them, and, depending on our needs and preferences, we determine what that sound means to us in a given environment. From this perspective, spectralism's ecological credo was born: "Music is what sound becomes."

The affordances and endowments of the musical environment hold vast potentials for what any listener might experience. Musical affordances, on a basic level, relate to elements like rhythm, pitch, harmony, timbre, and amplitude. These sounds are not abstractions but physical elements that live and die over time and in space. Yet the perception of these acoustic sound cannot be divorced from other aspects of the musical landscape, just as much a part of psychological reality, to which we become attuned in the process of orienting ourselves to our environment. Our perceptions are inextricably linked to our engagement with the variables of the setting, which include the sound's visual correlates and the physical attributes of the space. The myriad affordances of the environment address the complex identity and needs of each listener, which determine their perception. For we share an environment with sound, and our reaction to that environment directs our perceptions and reactions. From an ecological perspective, no sound approaches us neutrally. Music does not engage us in a vacuum; rather, how we receive any musical utterance is colored by the worldly particulars of our encounter.

Let's examine how, in practice, listeners might engage with the environments presented by two very different but related works, Zorn's *Cobra* and Haas's *In Vain*. I've chosen these compositions, in part, due to their similarities. *Cobra* and *In Vain* are partly aleatoric, partly improvised ensemble works with political leanings. Both were written by major living composers and claim extensive performance and recording histories. Stylistically, they differ in dramatic ways, yet they resist the labels of jazz and classical, notated and improvised, and tonal and atonal music—which at one time may have seemed useful to describing the musical experience but now seem as incongruous as distinguishing male and female as "opposite" sexes.

Cobra is an unpublished but often performed "game-piece." Designed to be performed by a group of improvising musicians and a prompter, and partly inspired by Stockhausen's *Plus-Minus* (1963/1974), the brief "score" (notecards, circulated in photocopies and readily available in the CD booklet and online) provides rules and cues and outlines modes of interaction among the performers. Categories include, for example, cues of Eye, Ear, Head, Mouth, Nose; Tactics (Imitate, Trade, Hold), Capture, Cross-Fade; Operations (Divisi, Intercut, Fencing); and Guerilla Systems. Any performance will feature certain kinds of rhythms, motives, harmonies, and other typically "musical" elements determined by the players onstage, but these change from performance to performance. Zorn was not intent on controlling the tonal, harmonic and rhythmic content of the work but rather in establishing an environment for collective noise-making which would acknowledge and exploit the identities and agency of the actors involved. He himself commented on his desire to harness the abilities of virtuoso improvisors in a semi-structured way. In "Ugly Beauty: John Zorn and the Politics of Postmodern Music," Kevin McNeilly maintains that *Cobra* thus radically privileges the status of the individual through its lack of a score, its dedication to communal music-making, and the relinquishment of compositional authority (McNeilly 1995).

Cobra is of an indeterminate length, but its drama and character emerge in a way that is far from random. As for the sound itself, it's traditionally noisy, brash, and chaotic and formatively influenced penchants of its performers, which may include pop, punk, heavy metal, jazz, television soundtracks, and sound effects. Due to its integral openness, *Cobra* is unabashedly eclectic, referential, and hybridized. In its realization, the work thrives on the intense interplay of performers and their instruments and the dynamics and forces of their interaction. Its kineticism is tied to this improvisational quality.

In performance, the listener learns about the workings of the environment by hearing and seeing what unfolds within it. What we learn about hearing and seeing *Cobra* realized is something about the freedoms it affords its performers, who alternately engage in dialogues, battles, and coups. As spectators, we witness its balances and equilibria and intuitively come to grasp what can and cannot happen in Zorn's world. It follows that if we enjoy witnessing this game unfold once, then we bring a certain knowledge of the environment to its next performance. That listeners follow the work and enjoy experiencing it more than once is evidenced by its rich performance history, which includes realizations by diverse groups of performers, including students (New England Conservatory, 2014), new music specialists (Kallio New Music Days, 2017), jazz luminaries (North Sea Jazz Festival, 2009), and an all-woman ensemble assembled for Zorn's "Women Visionaries: Inspirations from Hildegard of Bingen, Hilma af Klint, and Agnes Martin" (National Sawdust, 2018). To witness the realization of *Cobra* is to see the complex identities of its performers made manifest in sound.

Let's contrast this with a work that provides another kind of environment: Haas's *In Vain*. An hour-long composition for twenty-four players, *In Vain* features a harmonic language that reveals the influence of microtonal pioneers Ivan Wyschnegradsky (1893–1979) and Scelsi and the spectral composers Murail and Grisey, as well as American iconoclasts Harry Partch (1901–1974) and Tenney. Its sound materials are textured and fluid, with no explicit melodic or rhythmic thematicism. The environment is defined by continual glissandi, nuances of harmony and timbre, and subtle variations in density and complexity. In his notes, Haas evokes the Czech microtonalist Hába and his description of a music that is "free roaming without thematical coherence." *In Vain* also follows a dramatic program. Parts of the work are performed in total darkness, and these sections are improvised in a firmly guided fashion. The players memorize specific instructions, in lieu of notation, and respond spontaneously to one another in a highly choreographed fashion. Although denied visual communication with each other, the conductor, and the audience, they work collectively toward an ideal.

In terms of its acoustic language and theatricality, pre-determined length, and aesthetic orientation, *In Vain* is a breed apart from *Cobra*. While the environment of *Cobra* welcomes the viewer, who is invited to witness to its dynamic interplay of actions and reactions, *In Vain* denies its listeners this visual input. In this manner, *In Vain* recalls Haas's third string quartet *In iij. Noct* (2001), which is played entirely in the dark; both the quartet and the later work use darkness to overtly manipulate those actors in the environment, demanding that its listeners and performers attend to certain affordances by denying them access to others. There is a palpable violence to the work's stimuli, as the blinded listener is shocked into awareness. Yet Haas's listeners may be enthusiastic to be manipulated in this fashion. As Kevin McFarland, former cellist of the JACK quartet, notes, "The submissive person who is willingly giving over his or her agency can be getting precisely what he or she wants."

While Zorn's work has been identified with his leftist political leanings and is transgressive in the sense outlined by McNeilly, Haas's comes with a more explicit political subtext. He identifies *In Vain* as a protest against the rise of the Far Right in Germany. *In Vain* is also politically provocative in its evocation of BDSM, a topic the composer has discussed in relation to the dynamic that he maintains with his wife, Mollena Williams-Haas. (Ms. Williams-Haas is a woman of color and sex educator, as well as former International Ms. Leather, and their creative life was the subject of both the 2016 *New York Times* profile "A Composer and His Wife: Creativity Through Kink" and the 2018 documentary "The Artist and the Pervert.")

How dramatically our knowledge of either composers' politics or personal lives will influence our hearing of these works is not clear. What is certain, however, is that these very different works traffic in powerful energies and forces, addressing listeners as participants in different kinds of games and rituals. In *Cobra* and *In Vain*, physical factors, cultural references, and personal associations are correlates to the sound itself; they connect the sound to the specificities of the listener's body, identity, beliefs, and history. The listener may be enthralled by the dynamism of Zorn's musicians as they spontaneously confront and retaliate toward one another or captivated by the intricately choreographed actions of Haas's ensemble as they fulfill the constraints of its inevitable "plan." Yet how listeners engage with the sound of either work is driven, perhaps more so than any acoustic logic or pre-acquired "musical" knowledge, by aspects of their diverse identities and experiences.

> Culture and ideology are just as material (in the concreteness of the practices that embody them) as are the instrument and human body that generate this performance, and, as perceptual sources, they are just as much a part of the total environment. These are not "interpretations" drawn out of thin air and arbitrarily imposed on the music; they are specifications of the material relative to listeners enculturated in a particular context.
>
> (Clarke 2005, 61)

From the practical, ecological perspectives of the performer and new music presenter (rather than the standpoint of a cognitive psychologist), there is never a neutral level at which the listener is "just" receiving and processing music as an acoustic signal. Cognitive and identity diversity come into play even at the most elementals level of perception. These complexities are only compounded as we consider the levels of Performance and Project.

Performance

We can look now at the environment of the performance in which the sound is embedded. The nature of the setting—the actual environment in which the listener approaches the work for the first time, which is not defined by the work itself but those who present it—may have a tremendous impact on how any music is received. This context primes the listeners for physical, intellectual, and emotional engagement with sound; for social engagement with those who share their experience; and perceptual learning. Musicians often consider their choice of venue in relation to practical concerns, with an eye toward the size of the hall and number of seats, the cost of rental, and whether or not the venue will attract critical attention or even foot traffic. For someone such as myself, something as banal as whether or not the space actually has a piano is a critical factor. There can be real conflicts concerning what we believe is "right" for the piece, ideal for the performer, and most accessible to listeners. Yet those who present and perform new music must recognize the importance of this framing. In a world in which listeners have easy access to music via their laptops, i-phones, and other devices, the particulars of the Performance become ever more important. Those dedicated to drawing new audiences must consider how the environment enhances perceptual learning for the listener and make it a priority.

The environment of the performance determines how the performance is received. Clubs, art museums, and open-air performances possess varying degrees of formality, which attract different kinds of listenerships and encourage particular reactions. The standard concert hall brings with it protocols and expectations not only for how the audience is to behave but for how the performer is to behave as well. And we all engage differently with music, depending on whether it is presented in a space that has its own rituals (the concert hall, gallery, library, church, school) or not. That's why there is often a push to find non-traditional venues, such as the parks, airplane hangars, and abandoned turbine factories explored by NewAud or the garden along Philadelphia's Benjamin Franklin Parkway, where, in 2012, the Argento New Music Project presented chamber music of Murail and

Philippe Hurel (b. 1955). Alterative spaces encourage alternative, spontaneous behaviors.

Listeners' unique wants, needs, and preferences are reflected in the kinds of events they choose attend. Audiophiles may seek a pristine acoustic space, such as Disney Hall in Los Angeles, the Elbphilharmonie in Hamburg, or IRCAM's Espace du Projection. These settings provide them access to the kinds of sonic affordances to which they gravitate as listeners. Other listeners, seeking a more relaxed ambience, may prefer a venue in which they can have a drink while they listen, such as Chicago's Constellation or New York's (le) Poisson Rouge. Some want to smoke pot during the show. In 2014, the Colorado Symphony Orchestra provided this very opportunity to listeners with "Classically Cannabis," a four-part series designed not only to court its potential stoner base but, more significantly, to draw attention to issues confronting the state's legalized marijuana industry. Other listeners may prefer to experience music in spaces offering sensory input on more than one level, like an art gallery or natural setting; here, the aesthetic input may come from many sources. Some works themselves are designed for particular environments; composers whose music engages with particular spaces and places include Henry Brant (1913–2008) and John Luther Adams (b. 1953).

In his "In Search of an Ecology of Music," Adams discusses the relation of music to the larger environment.

> An ecosystem is a network of patterns, a complex multiplicity of elements that function together as a whole. I conceive of music in a similar way. For me the essence of music is not the specific patterns of harmony, melody, rhythm and timbre. It's the *totality* of the sound, the larger wholeness of the music. [. . .]
>
> After years composing music grounded metaphors of space and place, my music has now become more tangibly physical, in a small architectural space that resonates within a larger geographic place. . . . This is a space for hearing the unheard music of the world around us. The rhythms of sunlight and darkness, the phases of the moon, the seismic vibrations of the earth and the fluctuations of the earth's magnetic field all resonate within this space.

While it can be asserted theoretically that the autonomous work of art creates its own sonic environment, the ecological perspective recognizes the artefact as part of a complex system. The sound is just part of the performance, which has other crucial components and is itself subordinate to the larger project.

Project

To paraphrase Windsor and de Bézenac, real listeners do not just listen, and real music-makers do not just play. The experience of the listener is specified by far more that "just" the sound in the space. To understand their interaction and their impact, we need to look at the broader environment in which listening and performing take place and the extramusical processes that go into the effective presentation of new music. This is the scope of the project.

The environment of the sound, as I have ventured, is psychoacoustic: perceptual, mental, and emotional. It relates to the world inside the listener's head and the imaginative and creative experience. Perceptual learning that results from direct engagement. The environment of the performance frames this experience, contextualizing it within the constraints of the physical world. The variables of performance can enhance or sully the listener's experience of the sound and even prohibit access to the experience altogether. These two environments are closely linked. Yet the final level is that of the project, the complex system of interrelating actors who direct the enterprise. This overarching environment includes the performers, comprising everything from how they are treated and how they prepare to what they bring to the endeavor through their advocacy or lack thereof. This environment includes the artistic directors and those making programming choices, who are mindful of the concerns of performers and listeners, concert patrons, and production staff. It includes the administrators who decide on the principles that direct the organization and direct its goals, which direct how they approach audiences, composers, performers, and funders. It includes the press, community leaders, advocates, and critics. It can include rival ensembles. And it is here where diversity, identity, inclusion, and equity come into play most decisively as guiding principles. It is, I also suggest, the level least often considered by practicing musicians.

Those who control the environment for the performance determine how guiding principles are manifested in practice. The goals of the organization—this complex system in which the performance and its audience are nested—determine the means and the ends. If the goals are diversity, inclusivity, and equity, this is the environment where transformative change must be outlined.

To illustrate how a top-down commitment to creativity, diversity, and inclusion can have transformative effects, I'll consider "Julius Eastman: That Which Is Fundamental," the festival co-curated by Dustin Hurt, Artistic Director of the Philadelphia-based Bowerbird, and Tiona Nekkia McClodden. In the 2018–2019 season, "That

Which Is Fundamental" ran for several weeks in both Philadelphia and New York, paying unprecedented tribute to a figure marginalized since his death in 1990. For those unfamiliar with Eastman's biography (Levine Packer and Leach, 2015), it's worth reevaluating, not only for his contributions but to better comprehend how the choice to "revive" works of Eastman plays directly into current discussions of identity, ethnicity, and sexuality.

A gifted pianist, Eastman (1950–1990) studied with Mieczyslaw Horszowski at the Curtis Institute and gave his Town Hall debut in 1966. He had many talents as a performer and composer; as a vocalist, he is perhaps most known today for his extraordinary 1973 recording of Peter Maxwell Davies' *Eight Songs for a Mad King*, which he performed a few years later at Lincoln Center under Boulez. He was invited to join the Creative Associates at SUNY Buffalo's Center for the Creative and Performing arts, a program that provided residencies and stipends for performing artists and whose role was to bring experimental music to the community through its "Evenings for New Music" (1964–1980). Eastman was a founding member of the S.E.M. Ensemble and member of the Meredith Monk ensemble. For a brief period, he saw his works premiered throughout the United States and in Europe, including compositions with provocative titles such as *Crazy Nigger, Evil Nigger*, and *Gay Guerrilla*. Despite his historically momentous associations, Eastman struggled with his role in the avant-garde and his identity as a gay African-American composer. "What I am trying to achieve is to be what I am to the fullest," he said in a 1976 interview. "Black to the fullest, a musician to the fullest, a homosexual to the fullest." Eastman despaired over the lack of professional avenues open to him and became addicted to alcohol and drugs. Possibly a victim of the crack epidemic, he died homeless in 1990.

Bowerbird's fastidiously researched festival, three years in the making, featured performances of two works most performed during Eastman's lifetime—the pop-music inspired *Stay On It* (1973) and *Femenine* (1974)—as well as early works not heard since the 1970s, minimalist works from the late 1970s for open instrumentation, and late, more heavily atonal compositions. Performers included pianists Joseph Kubera, Dynasty Battles, Michelle Cann, and Adam Tendler; trombonist Christopher McIntyre; Bowerbird's resident Arcana ensemble; and Eastman's brother Gerry, a guitarist who toured with Count Basie, Sarah Vaughan, and Etta Jones. The festival brought Bowerbird extraordinary press and attendance and contributed to a revival of interest in Eastman's life and work.

"Part of the pleasure of Eastman's rediscovery," wrote *The New York Times* critic Zachary Woolfe, "has been the belated, deserving reinsertion of a Black, gay figure into music history." But Bowerbird's project was more than an attempt to simply include, as a token, a gay Black composer in the canon. Bowerbird's presentation of Eastman's music by musicians of color as well as white musicians was framed by events that recast the historical narrative of minimalism as more than the exclusive story of straight white men. It asked its audiences to consider the way we look at musical history and the way we relate to one another. In this environment, noted the *New Yorker*'s Alex Ross in his January 2017 review, Eastman's music became "absolutely, ferociously political."

"That Which Is Fundamental" sprang organically from Bowerbird's mission. Its institutional commitment has not only been to perform and present experimental, outsider, avant, unknown, and neglected musics but also to foster conversation and discovery. Its goal has been to cultivate communities of artists and audiences around powerful work. Hurt articulated his own ecological approach, recognizing the mutual relationship between Bowerbird and the local community to which it belongs.

> I see Bowerbird as part of an ecosystem and I'm always looking for ways in which we can contribute to the community overall. Fortunately, there's a vibrant arts community in Philadelphia, and lots of organizations doing great work. This gives me the opportunity to steer Bowerbird into the lesser navigated waters. We try not to needlessly duplicate the work of others, and we are always on the lookout for potential collaborations. I'm definitely in the "rising tide raises all boats" camp.
>
> (Hurt 2017)

Hurt's approach combines dedicated curatorial oversight with an agenda committed to cultivating strong relationships with the community. In the next chapter, I will return to "That Which Is Fundamental" and also consider the work of other performers and presenting organizations that demonstrate, more than mere lip-service or box-checking, honest institutional commitments to exploring issues of identity and place.

References

Borgo, David. "Free Jazz in the Classroom: An Ecological Approach to Music Education." *Jazz Perspectives* 1, no. 1 (2007): 61–88.

Clarke, Eric F. *Ways of Listening: An Ecological Approach to the Perception of Musical Meaning*. Oxford: Oxford University Press, 2005.

DeNora, Tia. *Music in Everyday Life*. Cambridge: Cambridge University Press, 2000.

Dibben, Nicola. "What Do We Hear When We Hear Music? Music Perception and Music Material." *Musicae Scientae 5*, no. 2 (2001): 161–94.

Heft, Harry. *Ecological Psychology in Context: James Gibson, Roger Barker, and the Legacy of William James's Radical Empiricism*. Mahwah, NJ: Lawrence Erlbaum and Associates, 2001.

Hurt, Dustin. "Inside Bowerbird: Q&A with Founder and Director Dustin Hurt." *Questions of Practice*. May 21, 2018. https://www.pewcenterarts.org/post/inside-bowerbird-qa-founder-and-director-dustin-hurt (Accessed May 23, 2019)

Levine Packer, Renée and Mary Jane Leach, eds. *Gay Guerrilla: Julius Eastman and His Music*. Rochester: University of Rochester Press, 2015.

McNeilly, Kevin. "Ugly Beauty: John Zorn and the Politics of Postmodern Music." *Postmodern Culture 5*, no. 2 (1995). Project MUSE. doi:10.1353/pmc.1995.0005.

Windsor, Luke, and Christophe de Bézenac. "Music and Affordances." *Musicae Scientae* 16, no. 1 (2012): 102–20.

4 Keeping It Real

As performing artists, presenters, and teachers, we define the principles, standards, and practices that can lead toward safeguarding and promoting cultural diversity and translate theory into practice. Every individual artist and organization has some capacity to raise awareness of contemporary issues regarding identity and diversity. We all have the potential to reach diverse communities and constituencies. Through the strategies we take toward performing, curating, and teaching, we can encourage the exchange of knowledge and best practices with regard to cultural pluralism, facilitating the inclusion and participation of listeners from varied cultural backgrounds. This, however, requires recognizing and encouraging the contribution that private individuals can make to enhance cultural diversity and establish forums for dialogue between the public and the private sectors. It requires that we come to a personal understanding how diversity and identity relate to our own endeavors. To this end, we must be specific. We must be pragmatic. And we must be real.

Be Specific

> We started this organization because we believed that making new music is a utopian act—that people needed to hear this music and they needed to hear it presented in the most persuasive way, with the best players, with the best programs, for the best listeners, in the best context.
>
> (Bang on a Can website)

The words above are a statement from the founders of Bang on a Can. With a slightly different inflection, they might have been articulated by Schönberg and Berg, whose goals for their short-lived society were not so different. Is one more of a success, one a failure?

I'm not sure this can be answered objectively, especially by me. In 1992, I co-founded a contemporary music performance group in New York with two composers, Jason Eckardt (b. 1971) and Alton Howe Clingan (1971–1996). Ensemble 21 was named for the upcoming century; it also referred to our ages at the time that we came up with the idea. We were first-year graduate students at Columbia University, new to the city, with many ideas and far fewer connections. The Group for Contemporary Music was in its final throes, as was Speculum Musicae, Parnassus, and other bastions of the uptown avant-garde to which we were drawn. Babbitt, Carter, and Shapey were commonly seen at concerts at Miller Theatre and Merkin Hall. Just that year, Shapey had notoriously been denied the Pulitzer Prize. The jury, which consisted of George Perle, Harvey Sollberger, and Roger Reynolds, had selected him as the winner, but the Board rejected their decision and awarded the prize instead to Wayne Peterson (b. 1927), asserting that "the layman's or consumer's point of view" ought to hold sway. I'd ventured downtown to the Kitchen to hear La Monte Young and seen John Cage explaining macrobiotic cooking techniques on late night television, but, five years after the founding of Bang on a Can, the rift between Uptown and Downtown was tangible.

Fifteen years later, our Ensemble disbanded, after having produced what were, for me, some of the most exciting concerts I'd been to in the city. We, too, tried to present new music in the way we found most persuasive, with the best players, the best programs, for the best listeners, in the best context. We staged a retrospective of the American experimentalist Salvatore Martirano (1927–1995), featuring the jazz singer Donald Smith and recreating the period piece *L's Ga for Gassed-Masked Politico, Helium Bomb, and Two Channel Tape* (1967). We were the first American ensemble to collaborate with IRCAM and presented the first American performances of music by Kaija Saariaho (b. 1958), Olga Neuwirth (b. 1968), and Jonathan Harvey (1939–2012); spectral composers Murail, Grisey, Hurel, Philippe Leroux (b. 1959), and Joshua Fineberg (b. 1969); and composers associated with the New Complexity. One of our final projects was the 2005 North American premiere of Ferneyhough's complete *Carcieri d'Invezione* cycle, a tremendous undertaking in which I'm still in thrall; "one could only look on in an incredulous stupor," wrote the critic Bruce Hodges. "Ensemble 21 can only be congratulated for a spectacularly exhausting night." We dedicated portrait length retrospectives to Stockhausen and Jean Barraqué (1928–1973). And while we performed more than our fair share of composers associated with the Uptown avant-garde—Mel Powell (1923–1998), Mario Davidovsky (b. 1934), and Donald Martino (1931–2005) as well as

Babbitt, Carter, and Wuorinen—we also played the music of young composers, some of whom we commissioned.

Ensemble 21 managed to attract audiences (even in the years before social media), good reviews, fairly reliable funding from government and private funders, and the valuable support of Miller Theatre and its Artistic Director George Steel. Yet as we became more successful and faced the demand for more and more impressive projects, we balked. We never had much of a plan, and we never intended to do more than put on our concerts, with the players that we loved and the composers we wanted to support, for the audiences that wanted to hear us. We didn't have much of a board, in terms of an ongoing financial support, nor did we have a vision for how to expand in a fiscally responsible way. Like so many freelancers, we moved from event to event, and only in the later years did we have the luxury to plan for more than one season at a time. We reveled in the creativity of our composers and provided our listeners with thoughtfully and sometimes innovatively curated experiences. After fifteen years, we had accomplished what we set out to accomplish musically, and our goals did not extend beyond that.

Our endeavor was immensely satisfying and rewarding and set a standard for performance to which I aspire to this day. But we never thought seriously about how to cultivate the largest or most diverse audience possible. We were not overtly concerned with issues of diversity or inclusion. We did not consider how we might enhance the access (except for people with disabilities, to whom we offered free seats), and we stayed in the kinds of halls to which we'd become accustomed, assuming that interested listeners would find us. Ours was just an attempt to realize our musical fantasies. And once we'd done that, exhausted by continual demands of time and energy, we moved on to new things. And the environment that had thrived around us instantly dissolved, like sugar in water.

Ours was one approach to music-making that, while immensely fulfilling and valuable as long as it lasted, was not sustainable. In retrospect, I see our failure in our inability (due to our own cultural blindness) to creatively find ways to bridge our own intensely dedicated, tightly bonded community with others. I am not certain we would ever have been able to bring the relatively esoteric projects we championed to anything approximating Cardew's "vast masses." But we did not, in hindsight, even consider this a possibility. We were content to play our music for kindred spirits, for those who were most like us and could already appreciate what we did. This attitude may have been bred into us, in our exclusive educations at the Eastman School and the Berklee College of Music. While we may have been devoted, in the abstract, to the "pillars" of creativity, diversity, and inclusion, we did not define those issues for ourselves in a way that could significantly affect anything regarding the scope and reach of our organization.

Today's ensembles and performers owe it to themselves to be more specific. The College Music Society's odd manifesto, in this sense, failed spectacularly by not making more of an attempt to define creativity, diversity, and inclusion. For it's necessary to define what these words mean to us first, personally and professionally. Then and only then can they influence how we can make our music matter in the world.

Be Pragmatic

It's imperative for performing organizations and individuals to acknowledge whether cultural diversity is, for them, a guiding principle (the means) or a fact (an end). Making this practical decision can help them determine how diversity factors meaningfully into their work and how it can bring about the results and bonuses they desire. There are differences between working toward social justice as a top priority, constructing a musical environment as a place to promulgate social change through music, and simply working toward enhanced earned income, which might be the result of more "butts in the seats." Diversity can contribute to both via different strategies.

The commitment toward diversity as an ethical responsibility can lead in many directions. It can encourage, from the top down, relationships with board members and co-curators who can create bridges to new communities. In 2015, developing the project that evolved into "That Which Is Fundamental," Dustin Hurt joined forces with not only with Mary Jane Leach, the composer who co-edited *Gay Guerilla*, but also Tiona Nekkia McClodden, the North Philadelphia-based conceptual artist and filmmaker. McClodden's work confronts issues of race, gender, and sexuality, examining shared values and beliefs within the African Diaspora and drawing attention to issues of inclusion and racial and social justice. Hurt recognized that McClodden's skills and perspectives, derived from her experience as a Black woman and artist, would enrich the project. "As a white straight man," he admitted in our conversation, "I felt really, if we were going to engage with those things, I couldn't do it justice."

As project manager, McClodden connected Hurt to other collaborators of whom he'd previously been unaware. Her rich social networks provided him access: a bridge to communities for whom Bowerbird's project had personal resonance. As co-curator, she designed a two-part exhibition featuring archival materials and works by ten contemporary artists. They included filmmaker Sondra Perry, who investigates digital technology's role in the systemic oppression of Black identity and the influence of Blackness on technology and image making; photographer Jonathan Gardenhire, whose work considers Black masculinity and its relation to constructions of power, value, knowledge, and social change; and Texas Isaiah, who creates photographic essays about legacies and empowerment, emotional justice, and the bonds between people and place. More than just a tribute to Eastman and his neglected contributions, the project used the examination of Eastman's life and music as a means to approach issues relevant to many intersecting communities and to bridge them.

Institutional commitments to diversity can also lead to the commissioning of new works that express ideas about social justice, with the goal of engaging disenfranchised communities. Projects of this nature include the Bavarian State Opera's *Moses* (2017), a multilingual opera designed for its youth program to address the immigration crisis. Combining music by jazz guitarist and composer Benedikt Brachtel (b. 1985) with excerpts from Rossini's *Mosè in Egitto*, its performers included refugees and children of immigrants alongside German children. It can lead to projects like Tania León's opera *Little Rock Nine*, based on a libretto by Thulani Davis, for which the literary critic and historian Henry Louis Gates served as historical consultant. Commissioned by the University of Central Arkansas, León's work commemorated the sixtieth anniversary of the Little Rock Crisis (1957) in which nine African-American students were prevented from entering the all-white Little Rock Central High School by the state's National Guard, upon orders of the state's staunchly pro-segregationist governor. On a smaller scale, it can lead to projects like pianist Marcus Ostermiller's recitals featuring composers such as Robert Savage (1951–1993) and Kevin Oldham (1960–1993), who died in the AIDS epidemic; programming Savage and Oldham's music next to that of Schubert, Ostermiller asks listeners to contemplate a neglected history of gay and closeted composers and the historical effects of diseases like syphilis on their musical community. Projects like these engage with current political and social themes, using the musical art to elucidate the issues at play.

For any performing arts institution, group, or dedicated individual, a determining commitment to social change can be a reason for being. With diversity as a guiding principle, ensembles, performers, and presenters can adopt strategies that emphasize music with political themes and provide opportunities for the audiences to respond. The idea is not to produce a form of agitprop nouveau but to present listeners with musics that engage provocatively with the issues of the day and offer an environment for discussion. "What we're doing . . . is nothing more than a narrative of that moment in history," explained León in a 2017 interview with Carmen Pelaez of NBC News, "but it has the possibility of starting a dialogue, which is what I would want—for us to have a sincere dialogue, not a cosmetic one."

Establishing a forum for dialogues on social and racial justice is core to the mission of The Dream Unfinished, the New York-based self-described "activist orchestra" founded in 2015 by educator and clarinetist Eun Lee. Its concert events have focused on themes of police brutality, the immigration crisis, race and gender expression, and the role of women in Black Lives Matter. The Dream Unfinished prioritizes programming composers of color, who have included George Walker (1922–1918), Vijay Iyer (b. 1971), Kareem Roustom (b. 1971), Courtney Bryan (b. 1982), Jessie Montgomery (b. 1981), and Huang Ruo (b. 1976). In bridging different communities, The Dream Unfinished allies itself with organizations including the Black Women's Blueprint, Center for Constitutional Rights, and African American Policy Forum. The agendas of these organizations have both informed the content of concert events and helped to bring them to communities for whom they hold personal resonance. Particular attention has been paid to providing access for populations traditionally underserved; performances in accepted venues for new music such as the DiMenna Center for Classical Music and Cooper Union have been supplemented by events at the Mount Morris Ascension Presbyterian Church (Central Harlem), Hostos Center for the Arts and Culture (The Bronx), and Museum of Women's Resistance (Brooklyn).

In all of these cases, the curatorial commitment to diversity and identity has determined the choice the programmed composers and works, the venue and contextualizing of the performance, and the overall scope of the project. Not vague nods toward notions of inclusion or equity, these performances and associated events feature musical works and personnel whose primary purpose is to bring provocative topics to the table hot. These projects appeal to the active and collective memory to which Finnissy referred, with the primary purpose of not only acknowledging and engaging with the identities and histories of their audience members but responding and adapting to them as well. Contextually, aesthetic concerns and performance virtuosity are a means to the end, in support of an overarching commitment to establish an environment designed to facilitate learning, dialogue, contemplation, and catharsis.

Not every organization or artist wants to affect social change by presenting music of political content. Promoting cultural diversity and social justice through repertoire choice need not be the primary goal. Some artists do not feel comfortable presenting programming that draws explicitly upon themes of race, ethnicity, or gender. (*The Guardian's* obituary for Ben Patterson, the Black Fluxus artist who retreated from the avant-garde world of the 1960s, described him as a cosmopolitan who "declined to be overdetermined by race.") Yet it's possible to promote social change without being a proponent of music that is in itself overtly political. Commitments to diversity may take other forms, which concern the bodies onstage as well as off.

Founded in Winston-Salem, the Gateways Music Festival (1993) upholds a mission to increase the visibility of classical musicians of African descent, provide role models, and inspire other musicians of African descent. The Festival was founded upon the idea that Black musicians playing music written by and played by performers of European heritage would cross racial lines and open up new audiences and career paths for young musicians. "Most people, when they think of African-Americans, they think of other genres, which are all phenomenal, gospel, jazz or blues," said the Reverend Robert Werth, a member of its board of directors. "But classical music is what it says: It's classical, it crosses races and it crosses ethnicities." Designed to provide an environment in which African-American performers of classical music could network, the Festival was proposed to function like family reunion for artists often isolated in regard to their race. In a 2017 feature in the local *Democrat and Chronicle*, it was described by Gino Fanelli as "celebrating a community of people rich with culture and a resounding artistic identity." Thus, the emphasis was on bonding within the African-American community and strengthening that community, rather than necessarily bridging to other disparate groups.

Since 1995, the Gateways Music Festival has been held biannually, supported by the Eastman School of Music. Concerts are free, and offerings in traditional venues are complemented by those held at houses of worship, schools, senior centers, and shelters. Performances by professional performers are supplemented by workshops, concerts, and master classes designed to nurture young performers. "Especially for our younger audiences of African descent, it suggests that this is something that they can do too," asserted the Festival's longtime chairman Paul Burgett (1946–2018), a Black violinist, member of the University of Rochester's Music Department, and author of *The Aesthetics of the Music of Black Americans*. "They can not only enjoy music at a very high level, but for some of them, they can see themselves as participants of this music." Burgett was forthright in asserting organizational goals that prioritized bonding within his community.

While some of the Festival's programming features lesser-known or neglected composers of African descent, such as Joseph Bologne,

Chevalier de Saint-Georges (1745–1799), and Adolphus Hailstork (b. 1941), many of its programs feature traditional classical fare. Yet it is most strongly distinguished by musicians onstage, where the image of African-Americans and their roles is refashioned. In this environment, the stage is peopled with bodies that many audience members are unaccustomed to seeing, making a music not always associated with their community.

In a similar vein, the Boston-based Castle of Our Skins, a collective led by violist Ashleigh Gordon and composer Anthony R. Green (b. 1984), was founded in 2013 to promote the music of Black Americans. Focusing on the breadth and depth of Black heritage and culture, the organization coordinates concert, educational, and community events, regularly hosting free events at the Museum of African-American History and meet-and-greet socials for musicians of color. In curated events, Castle of Our Skins collaborates not only with other musicians but also with organizations such as Chicago's Center for Black Music Research, poets, fashion designers, and visual and multimedia artists. Panel discussions regarding the activities of Black musicians in Europe have featured Chi-Chi Nwanoku, founder of the Chineke! Orchestra (the first European orchestra to feature a majority of Black and minority ethnic musicians), and Kira Thurman, a professor at the University of Michigan whose research explores the roles of Black musicians in classical music. The Castle of Our Skins also supports a composer-in-residence program.

David Myers, responding to the TFUMM manifesto ("Transforming Music Study From Its Foundations: A Manifesto for Progressive Change in the Undergraduate Preparation of Music Majors," 2014), proposed an ideal musical ecosystem that, by bridging the worlds of professional musicians, community musicians, and academia, would become "more relevant to societal concerns and thus more widely valued as a societal necessity." Organizations like Bowerbird, Gateways Music Festival, and Castle of Our Skins demonstrate how to secure that relevancy: by establishing safe environments that not only welcome diverse audiences but also provide for the honest discussion of complex contemporary issues of identity. These projects result from specific curatorial strategies, informed by research and tactically realized. They reflect profound institutional and individual commitments in support of their content. Music is but one component.

We can change the repertoire that we play in hopes of opening a dialogue, and this dialogue can be one that addresses aesthetic and philosophical concerns or topical issues such as women's rights, AIDS, immigration, and recreational drug use. We can change the faces and bodies of the musicians onstage, the conduits with whom our listeners will empathize in performance; who plays the music, in some environments, can be as significant the sound being heard. Finally, we can change the environments in which we play to provide access to listeners who would not otherwise be able to experience our work and to provide an experience that is transformative and encourages perceptual learning in a free atmosphere. Despite our passion for our work and even our confidence in our strategies, we must be aware of the tendency to preach. This is not about "converting" listeners to new music. If we want diverse audiences to thrive in the musical environments that we design, we must create environments that, more than anything else, afford them the opportunities to be themselves.

Be Real

Let's admit it: Some listeners may not be interested the new music that we are offering, no matter how well played, brilliantly conceived, or thoughtfully curated. While not being overly defeatist or pessimistic, we must resign ourselves to the fact that not all listeners will want to partake of our offerings. But this resignation demonstrates a respect for the identities and agency of all listeners, who come to their musical experiences with complex histories and tastes. Who they are influences how they orient themselves to the environment and also may determine their decision whether or not to keep listening. While some listeners may thrive and ultimately become part of our musical ecosystems, others may opt out. And if we have committed the same quality time to understanding our potential listeners as we have to our own missions and motivations, we will be able to appreciate and accept the complex realities of the situation.

Let's also recognize that not all forms of diversity produce tangible bonuses. Diversity can provide greater productivity and flexibility, and lead to innovation on many levels, but the presence of diversity alone does not guarantee any of these things.

> Diversity does not magically translate into benefits . . . it requires among other things that diversity is relevant—we cannot expect that adding a poet to a medical research team would enable them to find a cure for the common cold. Further, for diverse groups to function in practice, the people in the must get along. If not, the cognitive differences between them may be little more than disconnected silos of ideas and thoughts. Diversity like everything else (excepting, of course, moderation) has its limits.
>
> (Page 2007)

Sometimes, however, we do not recognize how vitally our work intersects with contemporary culture. If we do not grasp this ourselves, we will not be able to most effectively present our work to others.

With this in mind, I'd like to dissect a concert offered by the Lehigh University Very Modern Ensemble, known, for better or worse, by the acronym LUVME. This event is in no way a particularly egregious or extraordinary example of unspeakable practices. I have chosen it as an example because it is, to the contrary, so typical and exemplary of a specific problem inherent to much contemporary music presentation today: the inability of concert organizers to capitalize on the inherent richness of their projects. Thus, my critique is directed not toward the quality of the music or its musicians but toward a missed curatorial opportunity to fulfill the stated potentials of the project.

In Fall 2018, LUVME presented "The Irish and The Italian," a program that featured a roster of impressive performers, including soprano Jessica Bowers and pianist Blair McMillen, known for their performances of contemporary work, and the award-winning soprano Marisa Karchin. They were joined by the Dalí String Quartet, in-residence at Lehigh at the time and identified on its website with the tagline "Classical Roots, Latin Soul." Pre-concert publicity materials evoked a diverse program of "modern and traditional gems from both cultures" and "recent and not so recent music inspired by two distinguished cultures."

In considering diversity of assembly, there are many reasons why these particular cultures would be fascinating to compare and contrast on the same program, for they are connected by far more than the fact that both begin with an "I" and are "distinguished." The political and cultural experience of the Irish and Italians in the post-World War II era has resulted in fascinating body of musical, literary, dramatic, and philosophical work. This corpus reflects issues that concern us today: the fraught experiences of immigrants and persecuted minorities, the controversy surrounding the European Union, the rise of a significant authoritarian political class, terrorism and corruption, and religious conflicts involving the Catholic Church. How the LUVME program neglected to address the complexities of these identities reflects a missed opportunity for dialogue.

On this program, the concept of "The Irish" was represented solely by "Two Songs on Poems of Seamus Heaney" (2013), a setting by the American Louis Karchin (b. 1951). "The Italian" was represented by music of Giacomo Puccini (1858–1924) and Pierangelo Valtinoni (b. 1959); songs of Paul Salerni (b. 1951); and a quartet setting of the "Italian Serenade" (1887) by Hugo Wolf, the Austrian composer born in present-day Slovenia. Salerni is an American of Italian heritage, and

Valtinoni an Italian-born composer whom the publisher Boosey and Hawkes promotes by comparing favorably to the German Kurt Weill and the American Leonard Bernstein. Surely, complex issues of identity are at play. Yet these, in a "very modern" way, touch upon sensitive issues of nationalism, diaspora, and cultural appropriation.

Real identity is messy. Heaney was a quintessential poet of the twentieth century, yet it miscasts him to suggest that his words somehow exemplify "The Irish." And in what sense does the use of his words render Karchin's work an exploration of that purported identity? The composer's own introduction to these songs—written for the ensemble mise-en (New York), Ensemble Périphérie (University of Iowa), and Magnetic South (a collaboration between the University of Charleston and the Charleston Symphony Orchestra)—does not indicate that an exploration of "Irishness" was integral to their reason for being; Karchin describes the songs as "not ostensibly related to each other" and linked, rather, by a dramatic scenario of his own devising. We must similarly ask: What is there about Wolf's serenade that makes it any more "Italian" than Bach's "Italian" Concerto (1735), Mendelssohn-Bartholdy's Symphony No. 4 ("The Italian," 1833), or, for that matter, The Olive Garden? All concern affectations of an Italianate style and a passion for the Italian atmosphere—fascinating but, I suggest, far afield from the conception of a distinguished culture. Further, the documented inspiration for Wolf's serenade was a literary one: *Aus dem Leben eines Taugenichts* (From the Life of a Ne'er Do Well) by the Prussian poet Joseph von Eichendorff (1788–1857). (The main character in Eichendorff's novella is a violinist, and its plot features the performance of an Italian serenade.) Finally, one must ask, where does the "Latin soul" of the Dalí Quartet come into play in all of this? Neither the complex nature of contemporary Latin identity nor the rich aesthetic and history of what has been called "soul music" in a variety of contexts seems to be on the table for exploration. This vein of programming conveniently reduces of peoples to type. Its well-meaning aspirations to cultural diversity do not fully embrace or capitalize on the complex identities of those with whom they seek to engage. The Irish and Italian remain opaque, as do the equally complex identities of the hyphenated Americans on the program.

Schönberg's mentor Alexander von Zemlinsky (1871–1942) was deeply moved by the poetry of the Harlem Renaissance poets. He incorporated translated texts of Langston Hughes (1902–1967) into many of his works, including his *Zwölf Lieder*, Op. 27 (1935) and *Symphonische Gesänge*, Op. 20 (1929), the latter of which includes "Lied aus Dixieland" (Dixieland Song) and "Totes braunes Mädel" (The Dead Brown Girl). Does this make Zemlinsky a compelling representative of Black culture? Not exactly. Does it make his music interesting to perform in the context of Black Lives Matter? Absolutely. What we must recognize is how the music we perform relates to the environment, which includes the headlines to which we and our audiences wake every day.

The University environment is one in which students learn how to present music, curate programs, and critically understand new music's relationship to contemporary culture. As the TFUMM manifesto suggested, it's become a liability that many of our graduates have not learned how to how to situate their music-making in a position that underscores its social relevance. Yet we cannot do this, as educators, if the connections that we assert via our own programing conceits are not compelling. Ultimately, if we ourselves are not able to convey how vitally and naturally our work intersects with contemporary culture, we will not be able to present it compellingly to potential audiences.

By trial and error, we'll discover what diversities and identities best sustain the projects we envision. Over time, we'll see how diversity is relevant to the tasks at hand. And we will find ways to cultivate it, like a plant to be watered and fed, and to change our tactics with the seasons as our own organizations and practices evolve. In new music's ideal polycultural future, today's focus on creativity, diversity, and integration will increase the robustness and connectedness of our communities, resulting in hard-won bonuses for all involved.

Reference

Page, Scott E. *The Difference: How the Power of Diversity Creates Better Groups, Firms, Schools, and Societies.* Princeton: Princeton University Press, 2007.

Afterword
On Precarity and Sanctuary

"Precarious Sounds/Sounding Sanctuaries" was a February 2018 conference. Held at New York University, it was overseen by Assistant Professor Christine Dang, whose research explores topics including musical performance, politics, and religious identity in urban America. The graduate students who organized the event articulated their goals as a response to Trump-era government proposals.

> We are a diverse group of graduate student scholars, composers, and performers who came together to draft a call for papers and performances that address twin themes of precarity and sanctuary as they relate to sound. This conference comes out of discussion surrounding our department's support of the movement to create Sanctuary on our campus. This movement fights for material, legal, and emotional support for undocumented community members and for those affected by recent federal US travel restrictions. We hope for this conference to advance a nuanced conversation about precarity, sound, and sanctuary.
>
> (Conference website)

"Precarious Sounds/Sounding Sanctuary" featured presentations, exhibits, and performances. The three concert events featured composed and improvised works in a wide variety of styles, almost all of which confronted controversial topics. Performances addressed the suffering of Jews during the Holocaust (Olga Neuwirth's *In Nacht und Eis*), the experience of Jewish women of color (Leah King's *Mixed*), the career of the Internet activist Aaron Swartz (Dorian Wallace's *d4mn_k!d: intelligence boils down to curiosity*), and the American epidemic of gun violence (Drew Baker's *Age of the Deceased/Six Days in Chicago*). Concerts were packed and provided opportunities for audience members to vent about the disturbing political developments of the previous year regarding Deferred Action for Childhood Arrivals (DACA), Black Lives Matter, and the #MeToo movement.

At this conference, I performed *Stress Position* by Drew Baker (b. 1978), a work written in response to the torture of prisoners at the American military facility at Guantanamo Bay. I've performed the work many times, and over the years it has become more and more problematic for me. While it draws attention to a particularly ugly phenomenon and the brutality of American policies in the "war on terror," it also draws attention to the nagging question of whether or not music that aligns itself with activism makes a difference. In *Stress Position*, the pianist is required to repeat continually expanding chords in the outer reaches of the piano, with ever greater intensity, until the point of exhaustion. Amplification is used, and darkness as well, so that there is a sense of the oppression of the performer and audience members. It can be painful to play and hard to watch. Those in the audience may alternately empathize with the performer on stage and also find themselves in the role of the complicit voyeur, which may be its most compelling aspect.

Many listeners, including myself, find the work a sonically enjoyable experience, which minimizes its evocation of torture. The fact that the performer decides when to end the work similarly problematizes the work for me; while it does not exactly belittle the experience of torture, it offers the performer a welcome form of escape unavailable to those abused at Guantanamo. Listeners are also impressed by the virtuosity evident in the work's performance, but there is, of course, no equivalent "virtuosity of suffering" for which we can applaud the survivors of waterboarding or sexual humiliation. After performances, I have repeatedly asked myself what this work brings to the table but for my own precarity as an artist.

This question, and the many questions we have about how to position ourselves as musicians dedicated to new work in today's society, does not have an answer. To be meaningful and relevant, however, it does not need to. The questions that remain unanswered may be the most powerful, because they motivate the sincere dialogue that we want to be having, with those in our own bonded communities and those with whom we'd like to connect.

Having experienced the NYU conference as both an audience member and featured performer, I can attest to what could be construed as low production values, general chaos in seating, and something of a fly-by-night atmosphere. Roughness and enthusiasm at times overshadowed some of the more mundane and basic elements of production. Yet, when we venture into new territory, this is going to happen.

When musicians try new things and dare to strike while the iron is hot (in this case, responding as quickly as possible to what was perceived as an imminent political danger on campus), things can get messy. However, production values and concert ambience cannot always be our focus. Our technique is a means to an end, whether we choose to provide sanctuary for our listeners or remind them of the precariousness of their own positions. When Simon Rattle speaks of rethinking our conceptions of excellence, this is where we start: not with how we sound but with what we mean. For many performers, this may seem an undesirable trade-off. Yet in the construction of listening environments that are more robust and relevant, this is where we must begin. In the future, as our organizational commitments and personal missions become more refined through practice, we will do better. And then, it will not feel arbitrary, or inappropriate, to pursue a musical practice that looks both outward and in.

Appendix

America today is teeming with new music ensembles, most with flexible instrumentation and many with active commissioning, outreach, and education programs. Many of these groups move fluidly from the streets to the academy and back again. The oldest of these ensembles, which have been in existence since the late 1960s, continue to provide inspiration.

Taken together, they evidence the remarkable cognitive and identity diversity of contemporary music.

It would be naïve to suggest that these kinds ensembles do not fight for survival or that they do not routinely endure the trials of grant writing, fundraising, and administrative drudgery in its many forms. Yet their presence and endurance are testimony to the rich environments they have seeded and the communities that continue to nurture them. Their persistence disproves Henahan's assumption that "new music ensembles are like mayflies," and for that reason I note these organizations below with their year of founding. All remain active today.

Table 1.1 American Ensembles.

Ensemble/Presenting Organization	Foundation
Steve Reich and Musicians	1966
Philip Glass Ensemble	1968
Boston Musica Viva	1969
Da Capo Chamber Players	1970
S.E.M. Ensemble	1971
Collage New Music	1971
Percussion Group Cincinnati	1972
Kronos Quartet	1973

(Continued)

Table 1.1 (Continued)

Ensemble/Presenting Organization	Foundation
San Francisco Contemporary Chamber Players	1974
Dinosaur Annex	1975
Pittsburgh New Music Ensemble	1976
New York New Music Ensemble	1976
Washington Square Contemporary Music Society	1976
American Composers Orchestra	1977
San Diego New Music	1977
Relâche	1977
Newband	1977
Meredith Monk and Vocal Ensemble	1978
North/South Consonance	1980
Cleveland Chamber Symphony	1980
California EAR Unit	1981
Present Music	1983
PRISM Quartet	1984
Composers Concordance	1984
Network for New Music	1984
Cygnus Ensemble	1984
Earplay	1985
Orchestra 2001	1988
Talujon Percussion Quartet	1991
Boston Modern Orchestra Project	1996
Eighth Blackbird	1996
ETHEL	1998
Flux Quartet	1998
Nodus Ensemble	1998
Wet Ink Ensemble	1999
Sō Percussion	1999
Glass Farm Ensemble	2000
Argento New Music Project	2000
NOISE	2000
Fireworks	2000
Alarm Will Sound	2001
International Contemporary Ensemble	2001
Callithumpian Ensemble	2002
Either/Or	2004
American Modern Ensemble	2004
American Contemporary Music Ensemble (founded)	2004
Dal Niente	2005
Great Noise Ensemble	2005
Yarn/Wire	2005
Fifth House Ensemble	2005
Juventus New Music Ensemble	2005
Random Access Music	2005
JACK Quartet	2006
The Crossing	2007

Ensemble/Presenting Organization	Foundation
Found Sound Nation	2007
ECCE Ensemble	2008
Ensemble Signal	2008
Loadbang	2008
Talea	2008
Mivos Quartet	2008
Roomful of Teeth	2009
Asphalt Orchestra	2009
Spektral Quartet	2010
Seattle Modern Orchestra	2010
Chicago Modern Orchestra Project	2010
ensemble mise-en	2011
Sound Icon	2011
String Noise	2011
Sandbox Percussion	2011
andPlay	2012
Bearthoven	2013
Chamber Cartel	2013
Duo Noire	2015
The Dream Unfinished	2015
Ensemble Échappé	2015
No Exit	2015
Arcana	2016

Index